TOOLS FOR BIBLE STUDY
(And How to Use Them)

By

George H. Ramsey, Sr.

THE WARNER PRESS

Anderson, Indiana

Printed in the United States of America

20.07
183

Contents

This book,
written to help all readers
come to a fuller knowledge of the Word of God,
is dedicated
to my faithful wife of historic Bible name, Rachel.
I did not work fourteen years to get her,
but have worked more than double that
to keep her!
(See Genesis, Ch. 29)

Introduction

"The greatest book ever written"—every professed
Christian in the entire world would undoubtedly pay this
tribute to the book we have come to know as "The Holy
Bible." It has been accorded the accolade, "the world's
best seller." A great novelist, with thousands of volumes
in his library, spoke of it as "the book." Christians sing
in worship litanies that the Bible is "blessed book of the
ages."

But does this same professed Christian really *read* the
Bible? Do copies of this "best seller" remain unopened
and forgotten, collecting dust on some back shelf? Or do
we read the Bible from time to time for its "great literature"—here a classic poem, there a bit of priceless prose?
Or do we read the Bible only once a week in connection
with a church school lesson? Or do we dip into it from
time to time, coming up with a powerful "proof text" to
buttress a doctrinal decision?

Further, do we *understand* what we read? Does the
average Christian know what is meant by the warning of
Jesus that you do not put new wine into old bottles (see
Matthew 9:17)? Does he know why Jesus said, "If your
right hand offends you, cut it off" (Matt. 5:30)? Did
Jesus literally mean that? If a person interpreted this
literally, and performed the dreadful deed, would he not be
locked up for his own protection? Or again, what does the
text mean when it says, "render to Caesar what is Caesar's,
and to God what is God's"? (Matt. 22:21). Does Mr.

Everyman know who Caesar was? Or what we are to render to him? Or what entity in the modern world takes the place of Caesar? Again, when Jesus spoke of a "camel going through the eye of a needle" (Matt. 19:24), what did he mean? Is it therefore actually impossible for a rich man ever to be saved?

The above questions are a small sample of the numerous questions which could be asked to illustrate an important truth: readers of the Bible need some kind of guidelines for their study. They need a set of principles as a premise for their study. Certain facts must be known, certain standards of judgment exercised, or else the Bible becomes a monstrous book which confuses and divides men instead of enlightening and uniting them. These studies attempt a partial solution of the problem. They will be relatively brief and modest in their efforts, in the light of the vast knowledge available, but it is hoped they will give the reader of the Bible some help in setting up a system of intelligent and reverent Bible study. It is the writer's conviction that intelligence without reverence and reverence without intelligence both come wide of the desired mark for the seeker after God's truth. Jesus said of the Holy Spirit, "He will guide you into all the truth" (John 16:13), and the men to whom he spoke those words reverentially used their intelligence to learn the will of God. Let us do likewise.

There is basically only one way in which we may in reverential intelligence discover the great truths of the Bible, and this is by careful exegesis. This word is a synonym for interpretation, but it is more. Properly understood, the word gives some direction in the *aim* of Bible study and also some direction in its *method*. *Exegesis* comes from the Greek for *leading out*. The point is that

6

the reader of the Bible (and any other great literature) ought to seek two things: (1) to lead out of a passage the meaning which the original author (or spokesman) put in, and (2) lead out the meaning which the original readers of the book led out—if we can discover that meaning. (Of course, if the understanding of the passage by the original readers was perfect, the two points above are really one!) The opposite of *exegesis* is *eisegesis,* which means, *lead in.* And this is what we too often do with the Bible. We lead in to a text our own preconceived notion, doctrine, bias, slant, interpretation. We *impose* them upon the sacred text rather than properly *deriving* them from the text. We tell the author (of a biblical book) what we want him to say to us, rather than ask what he has to say. Leading in our own idea is eisegesis, and we ought to avoid it. Leading out the author's idea is exegesis, and we ought to practice it.

Let us illustrate. Suppose a skeptic wishes to convince a Christian that he ought not believe in God. He could actually quote the Bible in defense of his atheistic position. He could say, "The *Bible* says, 'Curse God and die' " (see Job 2:9). But this is eisegesis. *God* is not saying, "curse God and die." Job's wife is saying it, and Job rebuked her and kept his faith in God (see Job 2:10). The skeptic would be reading in (or leading in) his own idea into the book, rather than leading out through the principles of exegesis the meaning originally intended by the author. Or again, a mentally unbalanced person might read Matthew 5:30, take literally the words, "if your right hand offend you, cut it off," and cripple himself for life. But the intelligent person asks some questions: What was Jesus' purpose? Are his words to be taken literally or metaphorically? If metaphorically, on what grounds?

Do other passages of the Bible help answer these questions? The answer of course is that Jesus did very frequently speak in metaphors, that this custom was traditional and understandable with his Jewish audiences, and they would infer from his words, "get rid of the thing which causes you to sin," which of course is not the hand but the evil-spirited heart.

Seek, in the following pages, many truths contributory to interpreting the Bible, but seek above all the guidance of him who is "the Way, the Truth, the Life."

1
The Nature of the Bible

Our English word *Bible* has an interesting history. It begins with a city. The ancient city of Byblos (in Phoenicia) manufactured excellent papyrus. This papyrus was used for the writing of books (originally scrolls) and so led to the Greek word *biblos,* "book." The diminutive of *biblos* was *biblion,* and the plural was *biblia.*

So our word *Bible* comes from the Greek for "the books." Note well the plural. The Bible is a collection of books (as well as the Book).

But the Greek plural *biblia* passed into the Latin language as a singular, "book." (The Spanish title of the Bible is *La Biblia.*) So Christians have come to think of the Bible, a collection of sixty-six books (in the Protestant versions), as The Book.

Both of these ideas are important, and neither is to be emphasized to the exclusion of the other, as we shall note.

"Bible" Not Used in Scripture

Nowhere within the sixty-six books of the Bible do we find a reference to the *Bible* ("the Book"), applying this reference to the entire corpus (body) of the sixty-six themselves. The singular *book* is sometimes used to refer to a particular author's own book. See John 20:30, "Now Jesus did many other signs in the presence of the disciples, which are not written in this book." The author was referring only to his own book.

It is important to observe the significance of this fact in Revelation 22:18. The Revelator warned against adding to or taking from the words of this book. Some have taken this text out of its context (both literary and historical), and have taught: (1) By "this book" the author meant the Bible; (2) that Bible was the Authorized (King James) Version of 1611; and (3) twentieth century translations were therefore forbidden, coming under John's indictment. Of course John was referring to his own book, Revelation, not to the entire Bible, or parts of it.

Sometimes in the Bible the singular *book* is used for a collection of books which have a common motif or theme. Thus we read in Nehemiah 13:1, "On that day they read from the book of Moses." This did not refer to a single book but to a collection of books which the Jews attributed to Mosaic authorship (Genesis, Exodus, Leviticus, Numbers, Deuteronomy).

The Title "Scripture"

We also speak of the Bible, or parts thereof, as "Scripture" or "the Scriptures" or "the Holy Scriptures." The term comes from the Latin for *writing* (compare the English *inscription*). When capitalized the term usually connotes sacred writings and the writings thus identified depend upon the religious origin of the person using the terms. To the Hindu, the scriptures are the Rig Vedas, the Upanishads, the Bhagavad Gita, and so on. To the Muslim (Moslem) they are the books of the Qur'an (Koran). To the Jews, the scriptures indicate the thirty-nine books

10

we Protestant Christians call the Old Testament. To the Protestant, sixty-six books comprise the Scriptures, but the Roman Catholic will refer to a book containing these sixty-six plus the books called by Protestants The Apocrypha. So the term has different connotations and associations.

Use in the Bible

Nowhere in the Old Testament is the word *Scripture* (or *Scriptures*) employed to refer to the Old Testament as a body, nor even to refer to another Old Testament book. In later Jewish records the *Kethubim* (Hebrew for *writings*) came to refer not to the thirty-nine books of the canon, but only to the third section of the Hebrew Bible which followed the Law and Prophets—the section including such books as Daniel, the Psalms, Song of Solomon, and so on. The Greek for *Kethubim* was *Hagiographa* (the sacred writings or holy writings).

When used in the New Testament, *Scripture* or *the Scriptures* refers to some part of the Old Testament. Sometimes the word is used for the entire collection of Old Testament books. This was Paul's meaning when he wrote to Timothy, "All scripture is inspired by God and profitable for teaching, for reproof, for correction, and for training in righteousness" (2 Tim. 3:16). Some interpreters of the Bible have used this text to prove or point to the inspiration of the Bible, but Paul was clearly referring to the Old Testament. Note two facts: (1) Paul made the statement in a letter to Timothy. Other letters (or books) of what later came to be called the New Testament were not yet in existence. (2) We learn from verse 15 that Timothy had known the sacred writings from

11

childhood, and when Timothy was a child the earliest books of the New Testament had not been written. So by *Scripture,* Paul was referring to the Hebrew Bible (our Protestant Old Testament), or possibly to The Septuagint, a Greek translation containing The Apocrypha.

Jesus and the Scriptures

We noted previously that the term *Scripture* when used in a New Testament writing refers to an Old Testament writing or to the entire Old Testament. We cited 2 Timothy 3:16 (and context) as a case in point. The same usage occurs in John 5:39. The King James Version translates, "Search the scriptures, for in them ye think ye have eternal life." It is easy for the preacher or teacher to lift the three words "search the Scriptures," from their context and teach that Jesus was referring to the Bible. The RSV gives the correct translation (in context), "You search the Scriptures." and the "you" refers to the Pharisees, who indeed were noted for searching and expounding the pages of the Hebrew Bible (Old Testament).

Now note: when Jesus spoke these words, there *was no New Testament!* Jesus' words to the Pharisees are recorded in John's Gospel, but when Jesus actually spoke those words, there was no Gospel of John (or Mark, or Matthew, or Luke). Jesus was referring not to the Bible but to the Old Testament. And the further proof is in the context: "And it is they [the scriptures] that bear witness to me; yet you refuse to come to me that you may have life" (vv. 39-40). The context (and correct translation) make it plain that Jesus was urging the Jews to stop searching the "scriptures" (Old Testament) for eternal life, and to come to the Messiah to whom those scriptures pointed. Note well this passage, for we shall return to it for an important illustration in exegesis ("leading out" the meaning of scripture).

In this connection, note the New Testament usage of "it is written" which is equivalent to saying, "the scripture (O.T.) says." Note Matthew 4:4: "But he [Jesus] answered, 'It is written, "Man shall not live by bread alone." ' " As the reader can learn from the RSV footnote, Jesus was quoting Deuteronomy 8:3. (Many readers of the RSV do not use these footnotes, or marginal references, and they are important. The verse in the text above, as Matthew 4:4, is indicated in the RSV in blackface type. Then the Old Testament reference, or other New Testament reference, is given in lightface type, as Deuteronomy 8:3.)

The Word of God

The devout Christian calls his testament of faith not only the Bible, or Holy Scripture but the Word of God. There is a beautiful truth in this term, but sometimes the truth has been marred or covered by misinterpretation. Let us briefly examine some important facts. In the first place, the expression was used by Christ himself in referring to the Old Testament. He said to the Pharisees that they were "making void the *word of God* through . . . tradition" (Mark 7:13). As the context shows, Jesus was referring in particular to an evasion on the part of some Jews of the obligation of parental care (the fifth commandment) by a false claim of "Corban." (See commentary for details.) The Pharisees not only added tradition to the commands of the Old Testament, but sometimes their tradition nullified those commands. Our point here is that by "word of God" Jesus was referring to the Old Testament (compare John 5:39 on "scripture").

13

In the second place, the phrase "word of God" is used as equivalent to the gospel (the good news of what God did in Christ). Look at 2 Corinthians 2:17, "We are not, like so many, peddlers of *God's word;* but as men of sincerity, as commissioned by God, in the sight of God we speak in Christ." By "God's word" Paul did not here mean the Old Testament (although in other contexts he would quote it as God's word), but the gospel of Christ. We shall see in later studies that a Christian can get in real trouble by interpreting every word of the Old Testament as finally, fully, and infallibly God's present word to man because that "Old" Testament was preparatory for the "New" and the gospel of grace would supplant the warrant of works.

This equating of "God's word" with "gospel of Christ" can further be illustrated by Romans 10:17. The KJV translates late Greek manuscripts which have "faith cometh by hearing, and hearing by the word of God." The RSV has "preaching of Christ" instead of "word of God." "Blasphemy!" cries the fundamentalist, "they have taken away 'the word of God'. " But the facts are that the translators of 1946 have not taken away, they have *restored* what some of the oldest Greek manuscripts have, *"the word* [preaching] *of Christ."* The *word of Christ* came to mean, for Paul, more than the *word of Moses.* Paul once thought the word of Moses was finally and infallibly the word of God, but he came to accept Christ as God's final word to man.

Now note, in this connection, John 1:1, 14—"In the beginning was the Word, and the Word was with God, and the Word was God. . . . And the Word became flesh and dwelt among us, full of grace and truth; we have beheld his glory, glory as of the only Son from the Father."

And note the contrast in John 1:17, "The law was given through Moses; grace and truth came through Jesus Christ." Such exalted words as John 1:1, 14 were never written of Moses, yet the Jews considered the word of Moses to be the word of God. John the son of Zebedee had once so considered it, and so had Saul of Tarsus. Later both came to know that Jesus was the Word of God in a unique sense, and the Old Testament pointed forward to him. No single translation, but the teacher to whom all translations point, is, in the profoundest sense, "the Word of God."

Parts of the Bible

In earlier studies we have looked at the terms *Bible* and *Scripture* (or *the Scriptures*). Now we must turn our attention to two other terms used, in Christian nomenclature, for parts of the Bible; *Old Testament* and *New Testament*. Our English word *testament* is a transliteration (not translation) of the Latin *testamentum*. This was in turn a translation of the Greek *diatheke*. This Greek word could be used for a will—a document drawn to show a man's wishes for the disposition of his property after his death. The Latin *testamentum* could mean the same, and this usage has passed into English so that we now speak of a last will and testament. The author of the letter to the Hebrews used *diatheke* for "will" in Hebrews 9:16-17, which see. But a misleading inference could be drawn from this term: that God had died, and the Bible is simply his last will and testament to mankind.

We look therefore to the second meaning of *diatheke,* which is "covenant," and this puts us in the biblical perspective. The prophet Jeremiah had predicted (31:31) that God would make a new covenant (Hebrew, *berith*)

15

with the house of Israel, and this new covenant would be written not on tables of stone but in the hearts of men (v. 33). Jesus Christ, the Son of God, came to fulfill this new covenant, to be its mediator (Heb. 9:15), to be the new and perfect sacrifice to "put away sin" (Heb. 9:26). When Jesus spoke to his disciples at the Last Supper, he referred not to "blood of the new testament" (Matt. 26:28, KJV), but to the "blood of the covenant" (see RSV).

Some readers of the King James Version have inferred from the use of the term *new testament* in Matthew 26:28 that Jesus was referring to the document with twenty-seven books which we now call the New Testament. But of course no such document existed during the life and ministry of Jesus, and the correct translation "new covenant" helps us see the meaning of the passage. In accordance with this correct usage, note the title page of the New Testament in the RSV: *"The New Covenant,* commonly called The New Testament of our Lord and Savior Jesus Christ" (italics mine). The twenty-seven books we call the New Testament are therefore the records of the New Covenant.

The term *New Testament* implies a corresponding term, *Old Covenant.* In Protestant usage, this term includes the thirty-nine books beginning with Genesis and ending with Malachi (in our English version, Hebrew order different) which the Jewish rabbis approved in the Council of Jamnia (so-called) about A.D. 90. In Roman Catholic usage, the term includes the fourteen books Protestants refer to as the Apocrypha, containing such books as 1 and 2 Maccabees, Tobit, Bel and the Dragon, Ecclesiasticus, and so on. These books were in the Septuagint, the earliest Greek translation of the Old Testament, and were therefore valued and used much both by Jews and Christians in the first century.

16

When Jerome translated the Vulgate (major Latin translation, used in Roman Catholic scholarship as basis for several later versions), he included these books, but suggested they be segregated and called Apocrypha. He suggested it, but did not do so in the Vulgate, and so in Roman Catholic English versions today, these books are scattered through the other books of the Old Testament.

In excluding the books of the Apocrypha from the Protestant canon, early Protestant theologians had no intention of condemning the books. The books of the Apocrypha are very important from many aspects (historical, literary, religious), and should be read. They form an important bridge between the testaments. They give important background information on Jewish life and customs and ideology in the times of Jesus. This is not a plea for canonizing these books and treating them as of equal importance with such Old Testament books as Isaiah, Jeremiah, and Psalms. But the books should not go unread. The reader may secure a modern translation in the RSV, or may secure an edition of the RSV Bible which includes the Apocrypha.

Now note that the Old Testament (speaking from Protestant perspective of the thirty-nine books) is the record of the Old Covenant as the New Testament is the record of the New Covenant. It is a part of the Bible, but the implications of *old* and *new* covenants ought not be lost, as they are with so many readers. There is continuity between the covenants, but there is also discontinuity. There are many similarities, but there are important differences.

When Jeremiah (see 31:31) predicted a new covenant to be made with the house of Israel, he implied that the old covenant had not been perfect, and that the new would be better. Many Christians quote Matthew 5:17 out of its

17

context (we shall deal with this in a later study), implying that Jesus upheld every sentence in the Old Testament, treated every Old Testament pronouncement as perfect, infallible, and eternally binding. But in the very same sermon he said, "You have heard that it was said, 'An eye for an eye and a tooth for a tooth.' But I say to you, Do not resist one who is evil" (Matt. 5:38-39a).

The Unity and Diversity of the Bible

As you read the sixty-six books of the Bible (Protestant versions), note both diversity and unity. Look first at the diversity within the Old Testament itself. The first five books, Genesis through Deuteronomy, were attributed by the Jews to Moses, but later Jewish rabbis had to admit Moses could not have written Deuteronomy 34:6, where the death of Moses is described and the unknown author added, "but no man knows the place of his burial to this day." Who was that author? Jewish tradition says Joshua, but there is no documented evidence for this. Next we come to the Book of Joshua, but does the "of" in the title mean Joshua was its author or its hero?

The answer is probably found in the next book, the Book of Judges. This obviously means (and is confirmed by the reading of the book) that it was about the judges of Israel, not necessarily by them. The same is true of the Book of Ruth—Ruth is the heroine, not the authoress. The point is clear: many Old Testament books are anonymous (no name given within the book to indicate authorship). So as we read on in the Old Testament we find many books, by many authors, in many times, on many subjects, from many points of view.

In this brief study we can only suggest a few typical examples of this premise, but if the reader will carefully study these examples, discover more for himself, the point will become clear. Consider the subject of intermarriage. Nehemiah 13:23-31 makes it quite clear that Nehemiah violently opposed the intermarriage of Jews with other races. In fact, after his sermon against intermarriage, he confessed he "cursed them and beat some of them and pulled out their hair" (23:25). (Modern parishioners may be delighted their pastors do not follow up their sermons with such drastic action!)

Now go back and read the Book of Ruth. The record was obviously written by someone who approved of the marriage between Ruth the Moabitess and Boaz the Jew, and that couple whose love idyl is so beautifully and sympathetically told became the ancestors of David the great king! You cannot therefore legitimately generalize: the *Bible* teaches against (or for) intermarriage. You have to say that the author of Ruth favored it, the author of Nehemiah opposed it.

Or compare 2 Samuel 24:1-10 with 1 Chronicles 21:1-7. According to the account in Samuel, God himself incited David to take a census of Israel and Judah, and then condemned him for taking it. The later chronicler reports it quite differently, "Satan stood up against Israel, and incited David to number Israel" (1 Chron. 21:1). It is obvious that the author of 2 Samuel and the author of 1 Chronicles held different views on the subject of the inciter of the census.

Or take this question: Does God always prosper (in a physical way) his saints, and let sinners suffer? Many readers of the Bible would answer quickly (and dogmatically) in the affirmative, and they would prove this by saying, "Why, the Bible says. . . ." But then they quote one verse from the Bible, as from Psalm 1:3c which says, of the righteous man, "in all that he does, he prospers." But turn back to the book which precedes the Book of Psalms in the Old Testament, and you find the thesis of the Book of Job is just the opposite: God does not always prosper his saints, but sometimes tests their faith in times of adversity! So again we ought not to generalize and say, "The Bible says. . . ." but we ought to recognize the two diverse points of view.

Such examples can be multiplied by the hundreds, but that need not be done here. The careful reader of the Bible will discover diversities in point of view, doctrine, theological belief, historical remembrance. Some of these divergences are quite important and cannot be ignored.

But this is only part of the picture. It is also true that there is a most remarkable unity in the Bible. John the Revelator was referring in Revelation 22:18-19 to the same God of whom we read in Genesis 1:1, "In the beginning God." That God who so long ago purposed to bring life to man (read Genesis 1) labored hundreds of years later to bring eternal life through his Son (read John 3:16). This unity of the Bible (or continuity of the covenants) is beautifully illustrated in Hebrews 1:1-2a, "In many and various ways God spoke of old to our fathers by the prophets; but in these last days he has spoken to us by a Son."

The author of Hebrews certainly recognized discontinuities, differences between the two covenants, and the explicit purpose of his book was to show that the new covenant was "superior" (1:4, and frequently in the book). But it was the same God who spoke to Abraham, Isaac, Jacob, Moses, Isaiah, Jeremiah, and in the fullness of times (see Galatians 4:4) that God spoke supremely and superlatively through his Son. We may say there is one theme running like a golden thread through the Bible: The will of God for the world of God. We can understand that theme only by reading the entire Bible and by understanding the marvelous unity which transcends all diversities.

The Divine and the Human in the Bible

It is fitting that we now consider the divine and the human qualities to be found in this inspired writing. Let us begin with some obvious marks of humanity in the Bible. The Bible lying before you as you pursue this study is a book. It has, let us say, black print on white pages and is bound in black leather. Human beings felled the trees, made the paper, constructed the machinery, made the ink, killed the animals, dyed the skin, cut the pages, set the type, bound the book, and so on. God did not do all these things himself; he gave human agents the raw materials and the ingenuity to shape them. This is obvious, you say, but sometimes we overlook the obvious to our peril.

The title page of your Bible also indicates that it is a certain version, let us say the beloved King James Version. The title page goes on to say (in most editions) "translated out of the original tongues." Those "tongues" were languages, human languages, Hebrew and Aramaic (in the Old Testament) and Greek (in the New Testament). Although we call the book before us the Bible it confesses itself to be *"an* English version (translation) *of* the Bible."

Now ask: Who wrote those original tongues (languages)? When? Do we have the original manuscripts (handwritten documents) of the Hebrew text of Isaiah or the Greek text of Matthew? If so, where are they? What human hand holds them now? If not, what and where are the copies of the original manuscripts (*autographs* in technical parlance)? Who—what human—collected these

21

copies, compared them, made a printed text of them? To the thoughtful reader, all these (and more) questions are raised by the simple phrase, "translated out of the original tongues."

And who were the translators? What knowledge of Hebrew and Greek did they have? Now note the title page again: "and with the former translations diligently compared and revised." What former translations? Translated by whom? To what extent were the scholars of 1604-1611 (King James Version) indebted to these earlier translators? Why did they feel, in 1604, that a new version was needed? Did they understand that their work too would have to be amended as years went by, as earlier Hebrew and Greek manuscripts were discovered, and as more knowledge of these languages and of the people who spoke and wrote them came to the world?

Many of the above questions can be answered today by biblical scholars. The point here is simply that it is apparent that many human factors went into the making of the Bible (as a book). And what of the human beings who actually wrote those ancient manuscripts? Did they merely become passive automata, robots, dictaphones, transcribing in exact detail what God dictated? Some artistic illustrations in certain medieval manuscripts indicate this was their idea of the transmission of Scripture, but the facts say otherwise.

Had the author of every biblical book so perfectly taken down exact words (*ipsissima verba*) dictated by the Holy Spirit, we should not now have the discrepancies between 2 Samuel 24:1-10 and 1 Chronicles 21:1-7, referred to earlier. How can one say that the author of Nehemiah took down perfectly the words of the Spirit (conveying the will of God) on intermarriage, and that the author

22

of Ruth did the same, when the two authors come out in direct contradiction? Now note: this question does not deny the inspiration of the Bible (taught in 2 Timothy 3:16, with which we shall deal at length later), but only inadequate concepts of what is meant by "inspiration."

It is futile to claim infallibility for any human or any human enterprise. We Protestants (and an increasing number of Roman Catholics!) deny the doctrine of the infallibility of the Pope, but we have been guilty of claiming other types of infallibility (e.g. making a certain version of the Bible out to be a "paper pope") which are equally untenable.

It is clear that the Bible is, in many ways, a human book. But this does not at all rule out the divine element. Just as some fundamentalist authors claimed too much for the human element in the Bible, some liberal authors now claim too little for the divine! The pendulum of human ponderings has swung from the one extreme to the other. The truth lies in between: divine truths are couched in the Bible's human language.

Let us illustrate this by going again to Hebrews 1:1-2. The author clearly thought of the Old Testament worthies as inspired men (although he does not use this term, used by Paul in 2 Timothy 3:16), that is, God revealed something of his will and word through them. He did not, like the second-century heretic Marcion, find a "different God" in the Old Testament, and therefore throw the records of the old covenant away. He recognized their importance as legitimate attestations of a divine message. But note: he did not go on to treat those old covenant heroes as the final arbiters of the will of God; he did not put about their heads a false halo of infallibility. They led men to Christ, and Christ was the Revealer of the Father. Later on, we shall see this same theme of the divine through the human in Matthew 5:38, John 5:39, Galatians 3:24, 2 Timothy 3:15-16, and elsewhere.

The Interpreter and the Inquirer

If God entrusted the writing of his will to human agents, it follows that he entrusts the reading of his will to human agents. And just as there were many human helps in the writing—copying manuscripts, translating, printing—there will need to be many human helps in the reading and understanding of God's Word. There is a classic biblical illustration of this principle. The evangelist Philip asked the Ethiopian minister of Candace, "Do you understand what you are reading?" (A potential convert to the Lord, he was reading the prophet Isaiah.) The seeker replied, "How can I, unless some one guides me?" (Read Acts 8:26-40 for entire context.) God used the human agent to bring a part of his will into the world. He used human copyists to transmit and translate the Hebrew words. Now he would use a human interpreter and commentator to show his light to the darkened inquirer.

This principle of the interpreter (the scholar) helping the inquirer (the layman) is valid, but like many other valid principles it has been badly abused. The institutionalized Roman church of the Middle Ages set itself up as the absolute arbiter in (a) selecting the books of Scripture, (b) translating those books, (c) forbidding or suppressing other translations, (d) setting out formalized interpretations, (e) setting out formalized schemes of doctrine based on these commentaries, and (f) organizing the life of the Christian community, the church, around these iron regulations. The climax of this institutionalizing was the conciliar doctrine promulgated in 1870, that the Pope as "head of the church" and "vicar of Christ on earth" is the "paramount teacher of the faithful," and when he speaks *ex cathedra* (literally "from the chair," that is, in official capacity as Pope) his doctrines are "infallible." (The words and themes in quotation marks are denied by Protestants.) In later studies on biblical versions we shall look at some classic translations (actually mistranslations) and interpretations of the Roman church which believers are supposed to accept from the authority of the hierarchy.

Nor has Protestant history been free of such abuses. There can be (and have been) "Protestant pontificators" who imply that they have "the truth, the whole truth, nothing but the truth," and even "no one else has any truth." Suffice to say here that both Roman Catholic and Protestant theologies and practices have abused the principle of the interpreter helping the inquirer which we found in Acts 8. Philip knew much more about the Book of Isaiah than the Ethiopian official did, and he volunteered help in interpretation which would lead the inquirer to God in Christ. This ought to be the aim of every scholar, translator, interpreter, priest, pastor, minister of the gospel, or lay witness.

But note what Philip did not say and did not assume. He did not tell the convert that Isaiah was infallible and had all the will of God in one message. He did not say he himself was infallible, and had all the truth about the prophet. (We may add here that he did not even raise the issue of the authorship of chapters 40-66!) He did not set up a "school of thought" or an "Order of St. Philip" which would perforce follow in his every footstep and repeat his every opinion. At this point we ought to add: and neither did anyone else in the twenty-seven New Testament documents! Peter did not—astonishingly,

25

in the light of subsequent claims. Paul did not. No interpreter claimed perfection, infallibility, finality, ultimate authority. Later Christian commentators and theologians should have learned a great lesson from this simple passage, and we should learn a lesson from the fact that they did not!

In the sixteenth century Martin Luther set forth the doctrine of the "universal priesthood of believers." This briefly asserts that there cannot be a hierarchy of priests absolutely indispensable in informing the believer and in leading him to Christ, but that every man is a priest who can come directly to Christ in his penitence and be forgiven. Luther, and other Protestant reformers, based this premise upon such New Testament texts as Revelation 1:6, "Made us a kingdom, priests to his God" (the "us" refers to Christians), and Hebrews 4:16, "Let us then with confidence draw near to the throne of grace."

This Protestant principle, in its best and purest form, neither asserts that pastors are indispensable nor that they are unneeded. The pastor ought to study his Bible. If possible, he ought to study the original Hebrew and the original Greek, and be a competent judge of the merits and demerits of translations and commentaries and creeds. He ought to share his knowledge in humility of spirit with the unbeliever and with his brother believers. The pastor/teacher or the Christian/counselor/friend can be of great value to the inquirer, the Christian beginner, the listening learner. But no pastor, no priest, no professor has the right to absolutize, to infallibilize, to pontificate. Let us use, not abuse, the principle of the interpreter and the inquirer.

2

Methods of Bible Interpretation

The Device of the Six Ws

Students of journalism are taught that the opening sentences of an article in a newspaper ought quickly and clearly to answer the following questions: Who? What? Why? When? Where? To whom? We can call these the six Ws of information. For example: "John Jones was hit by a truck driven by James Smith yesterday morning at the corner of Fourth and Locust. The driver said he was blinded by the sun." We know, at least in part, who was involved, what happened, where and when it happened, and why.

We wrote in the previous section of the important Protestant principle of the priesthood of believers. This principle includes the right of the individual to have the Word of God in his own vernacular (at one time in history denied by the institutional church), and to serve—at least in part—as his own interpreter, letting God's Holy Spirit speak directly in the citadel of his own soul. There is a valid place for inquirer and interpreter, and each member of God's great church is interdependent with his brethren rather than independent from them, but ultimately God's Word to me, and to you, is a private matter.

Proponents of institutionalism argue that this leads to complete anarchy, and this is the fundamental Roman criticism of Protestant denominational and interpretational proliferation. With every man his own priest, and every man his own interpreter, chaos will result—this is the indictment. And we Protestants must admit that the principle of particularism, when abused, does indeed lead to distressing divisions. Is there a safer, saner ground between authoritarianism and anarchy? This writer believes there is. There can be enough study on the part of conscientious Christians, whatever their denominational background, that we can agree to a remarkable degree on a large body of factual material about the Bible, and then come to a basic unity (not uniformity) of biblical interpretation.

One way the Bible reader can work toward this end is to begin asking of every biblical passage the six Ws of interpretation: who, what, why, when, where, to whom? The reader will be amazed at the light which will be thrown upon Bible passages when he asks and studiously seeks to answer (with appropriate helps) these questions. Let us see how it works.

Who Is Speaking or Writing?

The first answer of the devout Christian is, "God is speaking! It is God's Word." In a very real sense this is true, and if it were not true thousands of scholars would not be giving their lives to interpreting and teaching this book. But we have seen in earlier sections of this study that the Bible is also human, written by men, translated by men, interpreted by men. We therefore need to ask of each passage in the Bible, Who (what man) wrote it? or Who (what man or woman) said so-and-so? To this question we address ourselves.

There are really two questions. One is, Who wrote the book of the Bible I am now studying? The other is, Within

28

the book, who is speaking, or who is being quoted? Take a case in point. A sentence in First Corinthians says, "Do not seek marriage" (1 Cor. 7:27). Now who is speaking to me? Is God telling me (if I am unmarried), Never get married? If every member of the first generation church so interpreted the passage, there would never have been a second generation church!

No, later interpreters of the Corinthian letter saw that the speaker (writer) was an apostle named Paul who, under a particular set of circumstances, at a certain time, in a certain place, counseled against (though he did not forbid) marriage. This writer believes that the Bible is the Word of God, that in a very real way God has spoken to him through the Corinthian letters, but when he was young and unmarried did not take Paul's word to the Corinthians as being in this case applicable!

Asking the question, Who wrote the book? or Who is speaking, as reported in the book? will keep the Bible reader from the old superstitious idea that since the Bible is "the Word of God" you can let it open at random, put your finger on a text, and that text is then the will of God for you. Suppose the Bible fell open at Job 2:9, "Curse God and die." It is not God speaking here; it is Job's wife, and she had lost her faith. Or again, in Matthew 4:6, "Throw yourself down [from the pinnacle of the temple]." A person foolish enough to have experimented with LSD might do exactly that, but in the Bible it was the word of Satan to our Lord, and the word was rebuked. Or perhaps the Bible falls open at the psalms, and surely here is "the Word of God"! But the text my finger falls upon might be Psalm 58:6, "O God, break the teeth in their mouths; tear out the fangs of the young lions, O Lord!" But this is David's prayer of vengeance upon his enemies, and our Lord has taught us to pray for the forgiveness of our enemies, not their destruction. It is always important to ask, Who is speaking or writing?

What Is the Speaker Saying?

A key question to ask now is, What is the author saying? The average reader of the King James Version will answer, "Why he is saying exactly what *the Bible* says he is saying." But it is not that simple. Remember that the word *version* means *translation* and in the Authorized (or King James) Version we have one English translation of the Bible. What does Martin Luther's German translation say? or the Spanish version? or other English versions, the Revised Standard, The New English Bible, and so on?

We spoke before of Christians being able to agree on a large body of factual material about the Bible. These brief studies can supply only a small portion of this valuable data, but these small portions are worth examining.

One fact of philology (language) and history is: in hundreds of instances, our twentieth century English versions (American Standard, Revised Standard, New English, and the many modern speech translations) are *more accurate translations* than the traditional King James Version. Some readers may feel like throwing this volume down in disgust over this statement. In Christian love and in the interest of truth, I ask you to read on with patience and prayer. My mother, to the day of her death, read devotedly from the Authorized Version, and it was from this version she first taught her little son. It was the version he heard when he found the Lord, when he dedicated to the Christian ministry, when he made his first feeble efforts at preaching God's grace. But I now know from my study of Hebrew and Greek, that the Authorized Version at many points does not render accurately the connotations of the original, and that some of our later translations do so render the meaning.

The lay reader wants to get as close as he can in English to what the biblical writers said in Hebrew, Aramaic, Greek. Without personal knowledge of these languages, he is dependent upon his English versions (or versions in the vernacular of his language, whatever it be). Therefore, one who wants to discover the truth should seek those translations which will bring him closer and closer to the very words and meanings of the biblical writers, and especially to the very words of his Lord! In the interest of truth, in the interest of unity, in the interest of a deeper walk in God's Word, the value of the new translations must be appreciated.

The reader is not being told the Authorized Version is without value. He is not being admonished to throw away his Bible of blessed memory. He is not being told that sinners can only come to the Lord and be saved as they hear Bible readings and sermons from the new translations. He is not being told that any one of the new versions is perfect. I am simply saying this: At hundreds of points the new versions come closer to the Hebrew and Greek of the Bible and give us clearer understanding of what the prophets, priests, kings of the old covenant, and Jesus—the Prophet-Priest-King of the new covenant— actually said. When the modern reader of the Bible in English asks the question, What did the author say? the new versions give him a better answer.

As a case in point, consider the AV rendering of King Agrippa's words to Paul in Acts 26:28: "Almost thou persuadest me to be a Christian." Thousands of evangelistic sermons have been preached from this time-honored translation, and we even have a famous hymn of invitation,

"Almost Persuaded," based on this translation. But the rendering of the Greek is incorrect. The Greek says literally, "with a little" you persuade me—and the "with a little" could refer to time or effort. Hence the RSV renders, "In a short time you think to make me a Christian!" The NEB paraphrases a little more, but still is closer than the AV, "You think it will not take much to win me over and make a Christian of me." The late Dr. A. T. Robertson, one of America's greatest scholars of the Greek New Testament, says of the AV rendering that it is "impossible."

The minister who has long preached from this text without knowing the Greek may be discomfited by the new, and correct, translation. There goes his sermon! But the answer is simple: choose a text of the New Testament which does indeed imply that a person is close to salvation, but that closeness is not enough. Such a text as Mark 12:34, Jesus' words to the scribe, "You are not far from the kingdom of God," would admirably suit. It is important to make the point to sinners that closeness is not enough, but we should not make the point from a text which in the original had no such connotation.

A second illustration is Galatians 3:24. According to the KJV, Paul told the Galatians that "the law" (of Moses) was their "schoolmaster" to bring them to Christ. For a long time this translation seemed correct. Paul's word in Greek (for schoolmaster) was *paidagogos* (literally child-leader), and from the fact that schoolmasters led children into knowledge there came into English the transliterated word *pedagogue* as a synonym for schoolmaster and *pedagogy* as a synonym for teaching.

It is now known (note: a fact, not a theory) by scholars that in Paul's day the Greek word *paidagogos* was normally used in the Koine for a slave, attendant, underling, whose responsibility it was to take the child to school, where he turned him over to the schoolmaster. He sometimes gave intermediate instruction (tutoring) to the child to prepare him for the work of the teacher. So Paul did not say to the Galatians, "the Torah (law) was the schoolmaster to lead us to Christ"—for then who was Christ? If the law was the teacher, what role does Christ play? Paul would not be guilty of leaving such an unbalanced analogy. Paul actually wrote, "the law was the slave (attendant, custodian, tutor) to lead us to Christ," with the implication that Christ is the teacher! You will find that our twentieth century translations agree on the basic premise, even when they use different (but synonymous) terms. The RSV has "custodian." The NEB has "kind of tutor." Today's English Version (TEV) has "instructor." Phillips has "strict governess." Goodspeed has "attendant." Moffatt has "held us as wards in discipline." The Amplified has "guardian . . . guide to Christ." Note that all seven of these agree against the KJV.

It is especially important that we see in the accurate version of Paul's words the inferiority of the old covenant, and the superiority of the new covenant. Many modern Christians are still perplexed as they read the Bible as to whether, and to what extent, the laws of the Old Testament are still binding. Paul gave the Galatians (and gives us) at least a partial answer when he used a well-known phenomenon of his age—the slave being in charge of the child until he turned him over to the teacher—to illustrate that the Old Testament was needed in Israel's "childhood," and has now led Israel to her teacher, Jesus the Messiah. When the teacher comes, the slave's authority ceases. The "tutor's" intermediate work is subsumed in the "teacher's" ultimate work. Again the correct translation is essential to the correct interpretation.

A third illustration is in Matthew 6:34, where the KJV translates Jesus as saying, "Take therefore no thought for the morrow." One can hardly imagine a more foolish, a less prudential, bit of advice than this: "take no thought for the morrow." This writer has told his Bible classes that if they take this advice seriously, and follow it, they will flunk the course! In order to pass a college course, work at one's employment, or do anything significant in life, one *must* take thought for the morrow! What is the answer? Did Jesus really give such impractical advice? The fact is that he did not. The Greek says, "Do not be anxious about tomorrow" (correctly translated in RSV and other modern versions). Now that is quite different, and a bit of practical advice which every Christian needs. Many physicians, psychologists, psychiatrists, tell us that worry about tomorrow is like a cancer, gnawing away at our insides. It would be improvident to say, "take no thought," but very important and practical to say, "do not be anxious."

A fourth illustration is 1 Thessalonians 5:22, where the KJV has Paul saying, "Abstain from all appearance of evil." Some pastors have accordingly preached that the Christian must not only abstain from evil, but from everything which to anyone might have the appearance of evil. This is, of course, impossible, for many actions not evil in themselves could be interpreted by others as appearing like evil. To illustrate: A Christian was seen coming through the swinging doors of a saloon, wiping his hand across his mouth as he exited. A spectator (and gossip) reported to a friend that this man had been drinking, and finally the report came to the pastor that the man was drunk! (So gossip grows in the galloping!) The pastor

34

knew his friend to be a total abstainer, so called him. It turned out that the man had been collecting money for the Community Chest campaign; he had solicited a contribution even in the saloon, and before exiting had bent to the water fountain for a cooling drink of water. Now note: that Christian coming out of that saloon was not (from the standpoint of traditional Christianity) avoiding the appearance of evil. But Paul did not say anything about the "appearance" of evil, he said, as in the RSV, "Abstain from every form of evil." The Greek says nothing about appearance!

Above are four illustrations of the importance of accurate translations. If space permitted, forty and even four hundred could be cited! This principle of biblical interpretation is clear: we should ask *what the author said*.

To Whom Is the Word Being Said?

The first two questions to be asked by the exegete (interpreter) are: Who is speaking? and What is he saying? We have considered in some detail the importance of these questions and have given a number of biblical illustrations.

The third question is also important: To whom is the word being spoken? To see the significance, reopen your Bible to John 5:39 and context. As noted in a previous study, Jesus was saying in the indicative mode, "You search the scriptures," not in the imperative mode, "Search the scriptures" (compare AV and RSV). Many interpreters, following the AV rendering as an imperative, have assumed that Jesus was speaking to his disciples. But ask the question, To whom was Jesus speaking? and then note how the context gives the answer. John 5:38 (the verse preceding) records Jesus as saying, "You do not have his word abiding in you, for you do not believe him whom he has sent." Note three occurrences of the pronoun *you*—note also the two marks of the persons to whom Jesus is speaking: (1) the word of God does not abide in them, and (2) they have refused God's Anointed. It is obvious these are not disciples, not Christians. (In contrast, note the marks of discipleship in John 17:8— the disciples had received Jesus' word and had believed he was the Christ.)

Return to the context of John 5:39. Continue to trace the thread of conversation back in the chapter until you come to verse 18: "The Jews sought all the more to kill him, because he not only broke the sabbath but also called God his Father, making himself equal with God." In verse 19 the "them" refers to the same stubborn Jews, and the "you" pronouns in the remainder of the passage (see John 5:25) continue that reference. When we finally come to John 5:39, therefore, we learn that Jesus is noting that the Jews do indeed "search the scriptures" (the Old Testament), but do not follow the lead of those scriptures as they "bear witness to (Christ)." Note verse 40: "Yet you refuse to come to me that you may have life." Correct translation and correct interpretation, employing principles of exegesis and considering the context, not only puts one verse or one paragraph in clear perspective, but also points in a significant way to the unique claim of Christ: he is the fulfillment of the prophecies of the Old Testament, and through him (rather than through Moses or the Torah or the prophets) God has truly brought eternal life to mankind. Many liberal theologians are today denying the unique claims of Christ, and sincere evangelicals must not overlook some of those claims through mistranslation and misinterpretation.

This question, To whom is the word being said, also throws light on such a text as 1 Corinthians 7:27: "Are you free from a wife? Do not seek marriage." Is the un-married man who is reading the Bible in the twentieth century to consider the pronoun "you" as directed to him-self? Is God the author of the commandment, "Do not seek marriage?" Upon some reflection, the answers are obvious. If second generation males had all taken Paul in absolute and universal implementation of the command-ment, there would have been no third generation of the church! The word *you* obviously referred to the Corin-thians, in a specific situation, at a specific time. The con-text makes clear that Paul was writing in view of "the impending distress" (1 Cor. 7:26), and this obviously referred to something in his day. Therefore the advice, "Do not get married," cannot be taken as the infallible word of God directed to all unmarried males in all nations of the world in every century!

A third illustration may be taken from the same New Testament book. In 1 Corinthians 11:5 Paul writes, "Any woman who prays or prophesies with her head unveiled dishonors her head—it is the same as if her head were shaven." "Any woman"—does this **mean** every woman, in every country of the earth, in every century? There are some communions in the twentieth century who try to ful-fill this text by insisting that women, if they are not wear-ing hats or scarves, at least drape a tiny handkerchief atop their heads before entering the sanctuary. But this is a far cry from the "veiling" of women referred to by Paul. Intelligent exegesis will again make it obvious that Paul's words were directed to a particular group of women in a particular situation.

Consider a fourth illustration. Paul wrote in Colossians 3:22, "Slaves, obey in everything those who are your earthly masters." To whom was Paul speaking? To slaves, in the literal (and horrible) sense of that word. (Paul used the metaphor "slave" of himself and other Christians—see Philippians 1:1, RSV margin—but in the Colossians passage he was speaking to men in actual subjugation to human masters.) Incredible as it may now seem, so-called Christian ministers long used this text in pulpits in the seventeenth and eighteenth century to justify the unthinkable practice of one portion of the human race treating another portion as though they were mere animals, beasts of burden. Paul was a great Christian, and bore magnificent witness to Jesus Christ. To read and learn from that witness, however, does not mean the modern Christian must follow the customs of Paul's day in minute detail.

Why Is the Word Being Said?

We have looked at three of the "Six Ws" of information, Who? What? and To whom? Now let us consider the fourth, Why?

It would seem that some people, when they were children, asked Why? too often, and now that they are adults, do not ask it often enough. At least in my experience, often in response to the question, "Now, *why* did Paul say that?" members of the class would say, "I never stopped to ask that question."

Read 1 Corinthians 8:13: "Therefore, if food is a cause of my brother's falling, I will never eat meat, lest I cause my brother to fall." I well remember this text because of an encounter with a very sincere Christian who was a vegetarian. Not only was he a vegetarian, he was convinced it was his mission to make vegetarians out of all his Christian brethren! So he quoted, "The Bible says, 'I will never eat meat'." He left out the portion, "If food is a cause of my brother's falling," and simply quoted the five

38

words, "I will never eat meat." Then he transferred the "I" from Paul to "God" and inferred that God had said, "You (Christians) must never eat meat." At that time I was making only twenty dollars a week in the ministry (first year in college). I tried to convince this brother I was already a "semivegetarian," not by religious preference but by economic necessity!

Of course the brother, sincere as he was, violated the canons of exegesis. He did not ask "who" was speaking or "to whom" or "why." Had he done so, he would have discovered (through consultation of a commentary) that in Corinth in Paul's day the meat supply of the city would have been offered in an idol's (god's) temple, but very conveniently, since the god had his fill and still left sixteen ounces to the pound of steak, the meat could then be sold in the marketplace. (In that kind of religion, you could have your cake and eat it too, or make your sacrifice and eat it too!) Some of the new converts in Corinth felt they would be participating in idol worship if they then ate the meat. Paul agreed with the more discerning brethren, "Food will not commend us to God. We are no worse off if we do not eat, and no better off if we do" (1 Cor. 8:8). After all, the idol had no real existence (v. 4), and the physical presence of the meat before the idol could not in any way contaminate it. Paul does not say he was a vegetarian, and encourages no one else to be. Only by taking five words ("I will never eat meat") out of context can we so interpret Paul.

But an important principle of Christian conduct is enunciated here. The "enlightened" Corinthians could not simply sit down to a steak dinner after asking, Is there anything wrong with my eating this meat? They would also have to ask, If I eat this meat in the presence of a "weak"

39

brother (one who thought it wrong), how will it affect him? Paul therefore warned, "If anyone sees you, a man of knowledge, at table in an idol's temple, might he not be encouraged, if his conscience is weak, to eat food offered to idols? And so by your knowledge this weak man is destroyed, the brother for whom Christ died" (1 Cor. 8:10-11). Then Paul gave his own practice and recommendation, "If food is a cause of my brother's falling, I will never eat meat" (v. 13). What a magnificent principle of Christian brotherhood! The actions of the wisest and strongest Christian ought to be in some sense regulated by his concern for the weaker brother, because Christ died also for that weaker brother!

But note another misinterpretation here. A Christian layman decided it was a sin for him to attend the Friday night high school football games because he would be associating with sinners. He then informed members of his Sunday school class that it was also a sin for them to attend. And he used the text quoted above from Corinthians with this application: "Your going to the games offends me, and you ought not offend me, and you therefore *must not* go to the games!" But Paul did not lay down the dictum that the entire behavior of every member of the congregation would be completely regulated by the conscience of the "weak" brother. This would be a strait-jacket religion of the family of Pharisaism. Paul was volunteering to regulate his own conduct, and recommending to the brethren that in certain circumstances they also follow this principle. (With regard to "certain circumstances": note that Paul specifically spoke of being seen "at table in an idol's temple"—he said nothing whatever about a man eating meat in the privacy of his own home, or in the company of men of like mind!) Our lives would be completely

40

"cabin'd, cribbed, and confined" if we let the "weaker" (less informed, less insightful, less discerning) members of a congregation draw up their own rules of conduct, and then categorically impose them upon the entire congregation! But the stronger members must also consider the weaker; however "far out" some of their ideas are, they are brethren for whom Christ died!

When Was the Word Written?

We have previously noted a very common misinterpretation of Paul's words to Timothy concerning "all scripture" (review the passage, 2 Timothy 3:15-16)—the assumption that Paul was referring to "the Bible" (all 66 books). This inference could be drawn from Paul's words only by failing to ask the question, When was Paul writing? To ask the question is to realize that Paul was writing a letter to Timothy, that letter was *later* regarded as a New Testament book, the letters and gospels previously written had not been collected into one volume (to our knowledge), and other New Testament documents were yet to be written. Therefore Paul could not have been referring to the New Testament books, singly or in collection. This is proved by the context, that Timothy "as a child" had been acquainted with the "sacred writings" (synonym for "scripture").

But when a teacher points out the above facts, some may draw the inference that he is therefore denying the "inspiration" of the New Testament. By no means! If Paul considered the Old Testament writings "inspired" (*theopneustos,* "God-breathed") as they predicted and prepared men for the coming of God's Son, would he not consider also inspired (perhaps "doubly inspired") those documents which actually reported the words and works of the

41

Savior? Saul the Pharisee had once considered the Torah (Law) of Moses not only inspired but inerrant and final (the two concepts are not identical). So he had believed it to be the will of God that men retaliate "life for life, eye for eye, tooth for tooth" (Exod. 21:23b-24a). But Paul the Christian came to see that "the law was our custodian [tutor, governess] until Christ came" (Gal. 3:24). So would he not consider "inspired" ("God-breathed") the words of Jesus recorded in Matthew 5:38-39, "You have heard that it was said, 'An eye for an eye and a tooth for a tooth.' But I say to you, Do not resist one who is evil. But if any one strikes you on the right cheek, turn to him the other also." If Paul considered the words of the "custodian" (Moses) inspired, how much more so would he consider the words of "the teacher, the Son of God"?

So a cardinal rule of interpretation is to ask When? Were the words under consideration part of the old covenant, or part of the new? Were they uttered by the "custodian" or by the Christ? Were they the words of prophets, priests, and kings, or were they the words of God's Anointed who is "prophet, priest, and king"?

Now return to 2 Timothy 3:15-16 and consider other facts which emerge as you ask the When question. We have established that when Paul wrote to Timothy the "scripture" to which he referred was the canon we now call the Old Testament. But exactly how many books were in that "canon" (Greek "rule," came to mean "list of inspired books") in A.D. 61-64? How many, according to rigid Jewish law? How many, according to common tradition? How many, according to Paul himself? Unfortunately, we cannot with certitude answer these questions.

Consider these facts. Many books had been written by Jews, in the intertestamental period in addition to the thirty-nine which we now call the Old Testament. Several of these books were in the Septuagint (a Greek translation of the Hebrew Old Testament), a version widely used in the Diaspora ("Dispersion") of the Jews across the Mediterranean world. (These books, usually numbered fourteen may be found in modern versions under the title "Apocrypha." Check one of the following: Smith-Goodspeed Bible with Apocrypha, Revised Standard Version with Apocrypha (also published separately), and New English Bible with Apocrypha (also published separately). These "apocryphal" books were excluded from the "canon" by Jewish scholars at the Council of Jamnia about A.D. 90-100. Now note that date: at least thirty years *after* Paul wrote to Timothy about "scripture" and "sacred writings."

When we ask the question, How many books did Paul regard as canonical? we cannot with certainty answer thirty-nine. We do know Paul sometimes quoted from the Septuagint, as being "the Bible" or "the Word of God," and the Septuagint included the books of the Apocrypha.

On the other hand, Paul nowhere quotes from or specifically alludes to a text which we now find in the Apocrypha. (It is interesting, in this connection, to note that the New Testament Book of Jude does indeed both quote from and allude to the apocryphal Book of Enoch and the Assumption of Moses—from the collection called the Pseudepigrapha (so-called because the authors used pseudonymns, names other than their own).

Now consider: had Timothy written Paul a letter in which he asked, In your opinion as a scholar of Judaism, how many (and which) books are in the Jewish Scriptures? and had Paul answered that letter, and if we had a copy of that letter in Greek (with English translation), we would then have the answer. But we have no copy of any such letter from Timothy to Paul, or of any such letter from Paul to Timothy, and therefore we cannot be dogmatic on the question, In A.D. 61, how did Paul stand on the question of the number and identity of the books in the Jewish Bible? Because this is true, many Christian scholars recommend the reading by Christians of the books of the Apocrypha, without necessarily putting these books on the same level as the thirty-nine books we call the Old Testament.

In the words spoken by Jesus to his Jewish antagonists, "You search the scriptures, because you think that in them you have eternal life" (John 5:39), we have learned that "scriptures" here refers to the Old Testament, because *when* Jesus uttered the challenge none of the books of the New Testament had yet been written. We learn in 2 Timothy 3:16 that Paul was referring to the Hebrew Bible (our Old Testament), because *when* he wrote to Timothy the letter he was then writing could not have been in a New Testament collection and other books of the New Testament had not been written.

Sometimes the question of when a book was written throws a flood of light upon a vexing social problem. A little over a hundred years ago, the terrible institution of slavery was still practiced in the United States. White men bought, owned, and sold Africans—sometimes separating families in callous unconcern. Even more callous was the attempt to justify this moral miasma from Scriptures of the *Christian* faith—the *Christian* faith, named after that loving Son of God who never uttered one word to justify human degradation! How was this blasphemy brought about? By twisting and perverting the Scriptures both of Old and New Testaments. They would read such a verse as 1 Corinthians 7:20-21, "Every one should remain in the state in which he was called. Were you a slave when called? Never mind." But as we ask the question, *When* did Paul write those words to the Corinthians? we realize it was a time when the entire Roman world practiced slavery, and Paul could not possibly have sought a complete social revolution. Words that were entirely appropriate for the first century would therefore be entirely inappropriate—and even blasphemous—for the nineteenth or twentieth centuries. Let us remember that Paul said in the same chapter, "Do not seek marriage" (v. 27), and nineteenth century white men did not take that as a command of the Lord!

The same principle applies to Colossians 3:22, "Slaves, obey in everything those who are your earthly masters." Since Paul could not have changed the institution so firmly locked into his age, he had to be content to ask both slave and master (Col. 4:1) to do the Christian thing. But notice also Colossians 3:10-11: "You . . . have put on the new nature, which is being renewed in knowledge after the image of its creator. Here there cannot be Greek and Jew, circumcised and uncircumcised, barbarian, Scythian, slave, free man, but Christ is all, and in all."

When men are saved, they take on a new nature. They are "born again." They are "new creatures" in Christ Jesus. They are in the "family of God." How could a white man rise from the altar where he had entered the family of God, and go back out into the world to oppress his black brother in Christ? He could do so in the name of human selfishness, or he could do so from a gross misinterpretation of Scripture, but he could not do so as a result of a word from or the spirit of the Lord Jesus Christ! Let us all pray in these days of great social tensions that men of all political persuasions, geographical distributions, denominational differences, racial origins, and economic strata *seek the mind of the Lord*. Not "black power" or "white power"—not the power of dynamite that blows up innocent children of all races, but the power of God!

Much the same can be said for the social evil of the subordination of woman to man. Not too many generations ago (with a few scattered throwbacks in our own day!) many men considered women to be inferior to themselves just because they were women! They were not granted equal opportunities for education or culture. They were not granted the franchise to vote for the men who would govern them. They could not enter the learned professions. In some denominations, they were excluded from the preaching-pastoral ministry, and in a few churches even excluded from teaching church school classes.

Now of course this was a form of slavery, much more subtle than the importation of plantation laborers, but slavery nonetheless. The evil was bad enough, but worse still was the attempted justification of such bigotry and prejudice by an appeal to Scripture! Many men who knew nothing of the words or spirit of the Sermon on the Mount could quote 1 Timothy 2:11-12: "Let a woman learn in silence with all submissiveness. I permit no woman to teach or to have authority over men; she is to keep silent." And note Paul's typical Jewish argument for this pushing of women to the periphery: "Adam was not deceived, but the woman was deceived and became a transgressor" (1 Tim. 2:14). Paul operated on the old Jewish premise that God would hold many succeeding generations responsible for the sins of one parent (see Exodus 20:5). However this principle was not only part of the old law, but an older part repudiated by the later prophets (see Jeremiah 31:29; Ezekiel 18:1-20).

46

Interpretation by Context

We have noted previously that a primary principle of exegesis (interpretation by "leading out" the meaning of the author) is to ask the twin questions: *What* has this author *said?* and *What* did he *mean?* (Readers of the Bible too often assume these two questions are identical, but they are not. Jesus *said,* "If your hand causes you to sin, cut it off" (Mark 9:43). But he *meant* (as we learn by the canons of Hebrew metaphor and hyperbole), "Shun the thing which causes you to sin."

A good translation can quickly tell you with a reasonable degree of accuracy what the speaker has said. (Future studies will take up the matter of the relative merits and demerits of the many English versions now available.) Frequently, however, we cannot tell what the speaker *meant* until we find out *what else* he said; in the same sentence, paragraph, chapter, book, or in other books he has written. This principle of exegesis is called "interpreting by *context.*" A single verse might be thought of as a "text," and the surrounding sentences or paragraphs form the "context." The importance of this principle is seen in the easily remembered maxim, "When you take a *text* out of its *context,* you turn it into a *pretext.*" This of course is "eisegesis," "reading into" the text the meaning you would like it to have.

If you will review some of the principles and illustrations of exegesis previously given, you will note we have already used the word *context* and employed the principles thereof a number of times. By way of review, turn again in your Bible to John 5:39. If you are using a version which correctly translates the indicative mode of the Greek ("you search the Scriptures," RSV, "you study the Scriptures," NEB), then you know *what Jesus said.* But you do not find out what he meant until you identify the persons to whom he is speaking (*"you* search"), and you do this by the context. You learn from verse 38 they did not have God's word "abiding" in them. You learn from verse 40 that they "refuse" to come to Christ. By tracing the context all the way back to verse 18, you learn he was speaking to the Jews who were seeking to kill him. This identity is indispensable to correct translation and interpretation.

Jesus was not commanding his disciples to read the Bible (the common interpretation), he was lamenting that the Jews were reading the Old Covenant in hopes of finding eternal life, when the books of the Old Testament pointed to the Messiah as the source of life! (Teachers, please note: it is of course a good thing to "search the Scriptures," and this is what we are about. But it is not a good thing to turn this text into a pretext by ignoring the context. Let us teach our students Jesus' original meaning, and then observe that it is only by *our* searching the Scriptures that we find the Lord.)

Consider a second text and its context. Temperance teachers and preachers quote Colossians 2:21, "Touch not, taste not; handle not" (KJV) as referring to spirituous liquors. They imply (or state boldly) that Paul was talking about intoxicating beverages, and that of these he said, "Touch not, taste not, handle not." Now that seems a built-in text for a broadside sermon! But note the context: Paul was asking the Colossians a question, "Wherefore if ye be dead with Christ from the rudiments of the world, *why,* as though living in the world, are ye subject to ordinances, (touch not; taste not; handle not; which all are to perish with the using;) after the commandments and doctrines of men?" (Col. 2:20-22, AV, italics mine). Paul

48

was not commanding an ordinance, "Do not touch, do not taste, do not handle." He was asking the Colossians why they submitted to such ordinances. Verses 20 and 22 put an entirely different perspective on verse 21, often taken out of context. If the student will consult a good commentary, he will find that the Colossian church was besieged by an influence some scholars call "incipient Gnosticism," in which extreme asceticism of food and drink was practiced as necessary to the Christian life. Paul was rebuking the Colossian Christians for submitting to their array of ascetic commandments. (But note: this is not to be taken as an approval of the use of intoxicating liquors. I have always proceeded on the premise that "the second drink will never cause you trouble if you never take the first." No man can tell whether he can handle alcohol until he experiments, and it is then often too late. Total abstinence—let us not mistakenly call it temperance—is still the best practice for the dedicated Christian, whose body is the temple of the Holy Spirit [1 Cor. 6:19] but it is un-Christian to seek to inculcate a good principle with a bad argument!)

To sum up: read the text in a good translation to get what the author *said*. Read, and reread, the context to help ascertain what the author meant. Try not to take a text out of its context and turn it into a pretext.

The Context of Covenant

We have learned that the Old Testament and the New Testament really ought to be thought of as the Old Covenant and the New Covenant. (See title page of the New Testament, RSV: "The New Covenant, commonly called the New Testament.") As we think of the exegetical principle of "interpreting by context" we ought not restrict this to the context of the sentence, the paragraph, the chapter, or even the book. Christians who seek to follow Jesus Christ as God and Savior (a commonly confessed creed) ought seriously to concern themselves with the question of "the context of covenant." We should ask ourselves the questions, What is meant by Old Covenant and New Covenant? Why is our Bible so divided? Are the two covenants unanimous in their teachings about God, about man, about sin, about salvation? Are the ethical standards of the Old Covenant the same as those of the New? Can the Christian be content to interpret God's Word by letting the Bible fall open by happenstance, put a finger by chance on a text, and take that as God's final word?

Many Christians ask few or none of these questions, but their answers are vital to our understanding of God's Holy Word. A failure to ask and answer these questions has led to perversions of interpretation, dividings among Christians, emphasis upon legalist observances, and the driving of many intelligent and educated people away from the church, and hence away from Christ.

To see the importance of interpreting by context of covenant, read carefully the following New Testament passages, note our summary of their significations, and check out these inferences *for yourself* by researching one or more New Testament commentaries.

1. Matthew 5:17-48
   a. Jesus promised to fulfill the Law (Torah), not destroy it.
   b. But note verses 21-48 where he amplifies his fulfilling of the law as follows:
      1) Part of the law, as "eye for eye," he repudiated.
      2) Part of the law, the great moral codes which

sustain decent and orderly civilization, he reinforced (such as the sixth and seventh commandments).

3) Those moral codes he reinforced he also reinterpreted— always on a deeper level of consciousness (motives as well as actions), and always eventuating in a higher ideal of conduct.

Consider, as one example, the paraphrase of Matthew 5:28 by Dr. William Barclay, "I tell you, if anyone looks at a woman in such a way as deliberately to awaken within himself the forbidden desire for her, he has already committed adultery with her in intention."

c. The strong contrast between "You have heard that it was said" (in the Old Testament), and "But *I* say to you" has been missed by too many sincere Christians far too long. Jesus did not put an imprimatur of finality or permanence on the teachings of Moses—let us see that straight and see it clear.

2. John 5:38-40
   a. Jesus was talking to Jews who thought salvation lay in the law.
   b. The Master said the Old Testament witnessed to him, and that salvation lay in himself.
   c. This claim was coupled with the firm assertion that he occupied a unique relation with the Father (see John 5:17-24).
   d. Moses had made no such claim, and Christ the Son of God could repudiate the premises of legalistic religion he was and is the "Son of God."

3. Galatians 3:24
   a. Paul did not say in Greek, "the law was our schoolmaster to bring us unto Christ" (KJV), but "the

51

law was our custodian" (RSV), "a kind of tutor" (NEB), "governess" (Phillips) until Christ came. The *paidagogos* prepared the child for the teacher; when the teacher came the tutor's job was done. The law was the tutor; Christ is the teacher.

b. The old covenant taught justification by works, but in Christ we are "justified by faith" (Gal. 2:16).

4. 2 Timothy 3:15-16

a. By "scriptures" (verse 16) or "sacred writings" (verse 15) Paul meant the Hebrew Bible.

b. Paul did not say the old covenant would save Timothy, but "instruct" him for salvation (RSV), which salvation came "through faith in Christ Jesus."

c. Paul's position here is absolutely consistent with that of Galatians 3:24, and consistent with his entire presentation of the Christian proclamation.

5. Hebrews 1:1-4

a. Note the contrasts between old and new covenants:

Old	New
1) earlier in time	1) later in time
2) came little by little	2) came once for all time
3) resulted in condemnation for sin	3) resulted in salvation from sin
4) accomplished through prophets	4) accomplished through The Prophet—Son of God

Summarizing Suggestions

We come now to the close of Part I of this study, where we have dealt at some length with the "methods of biblical interpretation," or "techniques of exegesis." Before going on to Part II, "Tools for Bible Interpretation," it will be good at this point to take a backward look and make some summarizing suggestions.

1. Review all the preceding segments, rereading with great care. Someone has said, "repetition is the mother of learning." I have found in years of teaching, that A. W. Blackwood was right when he said in homiletics class, "It is better to say the same thing twenty different ways than twenty different things one time each."

2. I have sat in Bible courses where we learned a great deal, from our books and from our professor, *about* the Bible, but we did not *study the Bible!* A great scholar once said, "The scripture is its own best interpreter." So search the Scriptures! Read and emulate the example of the Bible-reading Beroeans who examined the Scriptures daily to corroborate the preaching of the apostles (Acts 17:10-12). (The reader will remember that the Bible they read was the Jewish Bible, the Old Testament.) Many people read books on Bible study, read the author's conclusions, note in passing (but do not turn and read) the scripture references, and satisfy themselves that they have studied the Bible. Read. Reread. Compare versions. Challenge conclusions. Engage in dialogue with the writer of the book.

3. *When you have learned certain principles from one passage, test them out with other passages.* If you discover that great light is thrown on John 5:39 by the context, then be sure to consider the context in other passages which seem obscure. If a new version has helped you understand Galatians 3:24, it will help you understand hundreds of other texts.

4. *Pray for the illumination of the Holy Spirit.* Jesus said of the Paraclete (Greek "one called to one's side,"

53

used in John of the Holy Spirit), "he will teach you all things. . . . He will guide you into all the truth." (John 14:26; John 16:13). Note the singular *truth* (not all truths) and note the definite article *the* truth *(in the Greek but missing in the KJV)*. Jesus did not promise that the Holy Spirit would lead every Christian into all the truths in the world. No Christian in world history has ever been this knowledgeable! Nor did he promise that the Holy Spirit would give identical interpretations in identical constructions to all Christians, thus insuring absolute unanimity. Those who have so assumed have foolishly chased impossible fantasies, taken to themselves unreasonable powers, divided and disrupted the body of Christ. The apostles Paul and James arrived at no unanimity in expression, but they had marvelous unity in faith. Jesus did promise that the Holy Spirit would lead us into all *the truth*—the *kerygma,* God's saving proclamation, the *evangel,* God's good news that by his grace sinners can be redeemed. Reading truths (partial and proximate) in a study like this will lead you to the Bible, and it will lead you to the Son of God who called himself "the truth" (John 14:6), and the Son will lead you to the Father (Matthew 11:25-30; John 5:19-37).

5. *Recognize the revelation of God in the records of men.* We have said in an earlier study that in a very real sense, the Bible is the Word of God. In another very real sense, *Jesus* is the Word of God (John 1:1, 14), and the written words testify to the living Word. Jesus Christ is proclaimed in the New Testament as "the revelation" of the Father, and the New Testament writings themselves are records of that revelation. The writers of the New Testament claimed neither unanimity nor infallibility, but all of them claimed to be presenting *the kerygma* (mes-

sage, proclamation) of God's unique and sovereign Son, who alone is perfect Revealer of God the Father, and perfect Redeemer of man the son. We cannot ask the false and dichotomizing question, "Is the Bible divine or human?" It is both.

The principle abbreviated above, and spelled out in considerable detail in preceding segments, will help "Mr. or Mrs. Everyman" or "Mr. or Mrs. Every Christian" avoid extremes which today decimate effective Christian thought, worship, and witness. The biblical literalist who treats every word in the Bible as being on a par with Christ is actually negating the essence of the Christian faith at the same time he professes to uphold it! For the essence of the Christian faith is the unique authority of God's Son. We may read his words in many versions, and they will differ. But if we are convicted by the Spirit, the human words of any version will lead us in saving faith to the feet of the Son of God, and he will save us!

3
Versions

Importance of Tools

It is one thing to know what to do. It is another to have the proper tools and to know how to use them. It is not enough for the pastor or teacher to recommend, "Read the Bible." What Bible? What version? How do the versions differ, and why? If two versions contradict, is there a third tool one can bring in to throw light on the first two?

Part II of our study is devoted to the twin tasks of: (1) listing important tools of exegesis, with noted characteristics and (2) suggestions for using these tools in interpretation.

The first and most important tool of exegesis is one or more versions of the Bible.

Definition of Version

A *version* is a translation from one language to another. The thirty-nine books of the Old Testament were originally written in Hebrew (with several short passages in Aramaic, a "daughter" of Hebrew), and the twenty-seven books of the New Testament were written in Greek. Most, if not all, of Jesus' preaching was in Aramaic, and there are a few Aramaic words surviving in the earliest Gospel, Mark. We have no Aramaic manuscripts of the New Testament, however, which antedate our third and fourth century Greek copies. English versions purporting to be from the Aramaic are either: (1) translated from the "hypothesized" Aramaic word supposedly behind our Greek manuscripts, or (2) translations of the Syriac.

We learned earlier that the first technique of interpretation is to ask, "What does the scripture say?" Obviously the best way to find out is to read the Old Testament in the original Hebrew (or Aramaic) and the New Testament in the original Greek. But that is manifestly impossible (or highly improbable) for the average Christian layman. (Note: Persons studying for the Christian ministry, whether as pastors, teachers, missionaries, should if possible take at least two years of New Testament (Koine) Greek and at least two years of classical (biblical) Hebrew. What is the next best thing?

If you are dependent upon the English versions of the Bible, not knowing Hebrew or Greek, it obviously becomes extremely important for you to: (1) become acquainted with several versions, (2) learn something of the background and purpose of each, (3) acquire some standard of comparison between (among) versions, and (4) have some help in deciding which versions bring us closest to the words or intent of the original languages.

Before we proceed to these tasks, let us note one more definition. It is becoming increasingly common usage for speakers to equate "transliteration" with "translation." Pastors or teachers frequently make reference to "the Moffatt transliteration" (or Phillips, or Goodspeed) of the Bible. This usage is incorrect and should be abandoned. When we "transliterate" we merely change the letters from one alphabet to another. For example, *pater* is the English transliteration of a Greek word, but not a translation. The translation is "father." Transliteration gives only the letters of a word from a foreign language; translation gives you the meaning of that word. *En arche en ho logos* transliterates the first clause of John 1:1; "In the beginning was the Word" translates it. *Bereshith bara Elohim eth hashamayim we-eth ha-arets,* transliterates Genesis 1:1; "In the beginning God created the heavens and the earth" translates it.

There was a time in the memory of many who read these words when we spoke only of "the Bible," not of "versions" of the Bible. My mother never said to me, "Now, son, I am going to read to you from the Authorized (King James) Version of the Bible, translated A.D. 1611." Nor did she indicate that I should compare that version with the American Standard (Revised) Version of 1901. *Weymouth* and *Goodspeed* would have been foreign words to the young Sunday school scholar! A mother or father, Sunday school teacher or pastor, would simply speak— in most cases—of "the Bible," and the reference was to the Authorized Version.

Now we not only have several English versions in our bookstores, libraries, churches, homes, but what some regard as a bewildering array of versions. There is a smorgasbord of translation! How does one decide? A variety of versions, a treasure of translations—how does the Christian layman (or minister who has not studied Greek and Hebrew) decide among them? In such a dilemma, it is easy to fall into extremes. One extreme would be to consider the Authorized Version (without valid evidence or premises) as the Bible, and repudiate all other versions. The other extreme would be to read any or all as equally valid, equally important, translated from identical premises. There is great peril, or there are many problems, in both these approaches.

Next, we shall look at a "categorizing of versions" which will give some guidance to the merits and demerits, advantages and disadvantages, of the numerous Bible versions available.

Categories of English Versions

I have worked out a number of "categories of versions" with certain appropriate criteria (standards of evaluation) for each. This "table of categories" has been used in college Bible courses, courses for ministers, courses for laymen in conventions, camp meetings, conferences. Please note: no claim of perfection or finality is made for these categories, and for each "rule" there will be exceptions, which cannot always be spelled out. But certain facts are clear, certain comparisons are inevitable, and certain conclusions are widely agreed upon among biblical scholars and laymen should have this information in clear form.

We propose to divide the English versions available today into three basic categories: (1) *the standard versions,* (2) *the modern speech versions,* and (3) *the combination versions.* We shall examine the major English versions (selective, not exhaustive) in the three categories, and then list the criteria by which they are so assigned.

Category I: The Standard Versions
   a. AV—The Authorized Version also called the KJV—The King James Version (1611)
   b. ERV—English Revised Version (1881, 1885)
   c. ASV—American Standard Version, also called the ARV—American Revised Version (1901) based on ERV.
   d. RSV—Revised Standard Version (1946, 1952)
   e. NASV—New American Standard Version (1960-63)
   f. NEB—New English Bible (1961, 1970)

Notes: (1) The Bible student should familiarize himself with the abbreviations, for they are frequently used in a wide variety of publications. (2) Where two dates are given, the first refers to the publication of the New Testament, the second the Old Testament. (3) Observe that three of the translations have the word *standard* in the title; hence our use of this word for this category. (4) Observe that the ASV, RSV, and NEB are all twentieth-century translations, the ERV nineteenth century, the AV seventeenth century. The significance of this fact will appear later in this study.

Category II: The Modern Speech Versions

A partial listing of the many modern speech versions follows: Listed in alphabetical order by translator.

Barclay, William, *The New Testament* (Vol. I, Gospels and Acts, Vol. II, The Letters and the Revelation)

Bratcher, Robert, *Today's English Version* (abbrev. TEV), also known as *Good News for Modern Man*

Goodspeed, Edgar, *The New Testament, An American Translation*

Knox, Ronald, *The New Testament; A New Translation*

Moffatt, James, *The Bible*

Phillips, J. B., *The New Testament in Modern English*

Taylor, Kenneth, *The Living New Testament* also portions, *Living Gospels, Living Letters*

Weymouth, Richard, *The New Testament in Modern Speech*

Williams, Charles, *The New Testament in the Language of the People*

Category III: The Combination Versions

The best example is *The Amplified Bible*. It partakes, as will be developed later, of some of the qualities of the standard translations and some of the qualities of the modern speech translations.

The Criteria of the Categories

Some years ago a minister said, "As I prepare my sermons, I read from five versions of the Bible, pick out the one I like the best, and preach from that one." In the context of the conversation he was not confessing the sparseness of his sermon preparation, but complimenting its amplitude! Now note the catch here: "pick out the one I like the best." The one he liked the best, which fit in comfortably with his traditions, predilections, convictions, may have been the farthest of the five from the literal meaning of the original! And without the original, or some work in commentaries, he could not tell!

Many ministers and laymen are using the modern speech versions (Phillips, Goodspeed, etc.) as though there were no difference between them and the standard versions, as though any one is automatically as good as any other, as though all were translated from exactly the same premises and presuppositions. This assumption is misleading and dangerous. There are certain rather important differences between the two categories, standard and modern speech, and Bible students should recognize them.

The *two major criteria* of the categories are these:

1. The standard versions (AV, ERV, ASV, RSV, NEB) were translated by committees of scholars, while the modern speech versions were translated by individuals, (Phillips, Moffatt, Goodspeed, etc.).

61

2. The standard versions are generally (note the limiting adverb) more *literal translations,* while the modern speech versions resort much more often to *paraphrase.*

Let us note some of the implications of these two different types of translations:

Standard—Committee   Modern Speech—Individual

a) The AV was translated by a committee of 54 scholars, all from the Church of England. The work was "authorized" by James I, King of England, and head of the Anglican Church.

b) The ASV was translated by a committee of scholars, drawn from a cross section of American denominations.

c) The RSV was likewise translated by a committee of scholars, drawn from a wide distribution of American denominations. The names of the scholars and something of their background will be found in the pamphlet, *An Introduction to the Revised Standard Version of the New Testament* (similar pamphlet for OT).

d) The NEB, completed in March, 1970, was made by a committee representing several British denominations (listed opposite the title page). The preface of the NEB explains in brief the work of the three panels.

e) Now it should be obvious that a version made by a committee of reputable scholars, drawn from a cross section of churches, with geographical and age distribution, agreeing by two-thirds majority on the rendering of the Hebrew and the Greek, is likely to be more important, more solid, more "secure" than a version made, as in the case of the modern speech, by one scholar only. The Scripture itself says, "in an abundance of counselors there is safety" (Prov. 11:14b).

The single translator puts his own ideas into his version, and this is proper. But the "single vote version" ought not be considered as equal to, on a par with, as stable as, the version where a system of "checks and balances" has been put into effect.

The following hypothetical case illustrates the point. Suppose a scholar from a denomination which practices infant baptism (by sprinkling) tried to intrude his theology into the translation by rendering the Greek *baptizo* as "sprinkle." (No scholar would propose such a thing, for scholars in churches where sprinkling is practiced generally agree the Greek *bapto* meant "the dip" and recognize the clear cases of immersion—as Acts 8:38-39.) If he did, his brother from an "immersionist" church, seated across the table, would demur, and the issue would be put to committee vote.

f) On the other hand, it is only fair to admit that an excellent translation might get only minority vote in committee, and the proposer of that translation has every right to publish it. I share the view of Dr. James Moffatt that there has been a "dislocation" in the order of the verses in Romans 7, and that verse 25b makes no sense in the present order and a great deal of sense when transposed to follow verse 23. (Study the passage, and read commentary materials, to see the nature of the problem.) But such a proposal has not carried in any of the major committee projects, the standard translations.

g) To sum up, it is better for Bible students to give heavier weight, as a rule, to standard translations (especially those of the twentieth century) and use the modern speech versions to supplement and complement them. A second reason for this will soon be obvious.

Standard—More Literal Translation

Modern Speech—Paraphrase

a) Definitions of "literal" and "paraphrase": The literal translation says more nearly in English what the Greek (or Hebrew) says. It stays closer to the very words of the original. The paraphrase takes the gist of the idea in the original, then renders it very freely into English.

b) Examples of literal and paraphrase.

Compare Galatians 3:1 in a standard version (RSV) and a modern speech version (Phillips). The RSV renders the Greek literally, "O foolish Galatians!" J. B. Phillips translates, "O my dear idiots." This latter is very intriguing. I have read aloud to many study groups, "O foolish Galatians!" and got no response. But when I read, "O my dear idiots," there were smiles, appreciative chuckles, even laughs! Phillips captures the attention, the imagination.

Interesting as the translation is, there is no word in Greek for "dear." The Phillips version is not a literal translation, but a paraphrase. But the paraphrase is justified by the fact that the Galatians are indeed dear to Paul. We shall expand later on the note: a *paraphrase* is one step in the direction of a *commentary*.

A fuller and more ample illustration of the difference between the standard (literal) version and the modern speech (paraphrased) version is seen in Matthew 5:27-28, (AV). "Ye have heard that it was said by them of old time, Thou shalt not commit adultery: But I say unto you, That whosoever looketh on a woman to lust after her hath committed adultery with her already in his heart." The RSV and NEB follow this rendering very closely, except they remove the archaic expressions "Ye," "thou shalt not," and so on. The AV, RSV, NEB are all literal, they render the Greek almost word for word.

Now note the William Barclay rendering: "But I say to you, that every one who looks at a woman in such a way as deliberately to awaken within himself forbidden desires for her has already committed adultery with her within his heart." Now it is obvious to anyone that this translation is greatly expanded. It will probably not be obvious that the Greek has no word for "deliberately" or "awaken within himself." But as we said earlier on the Phillips rendition of Galatians 3:1, it is a "justified paraphrase." It faithfully represents Jesus' meaning, and expresses it in striking English phraseology.

The major problem with the paraphrase is that the minister or layman who does not know Greek is likely to put too much stress on a single word of the English translation (as, in the case above, the word "deliberately") when that word is not even in the Greek. The NEB, for example, even though a standard version, resorts *much more to paraphrase* than the RSV, and sometimes this can be misleading.

Consider 1 Corinthians 14:2, "He that speaketh in an unknown tongue speaketh not unto men but unto God" (AV). Certain interpreters tell their people the adjective "unknown" is italicized for emphasis, when in reality italics in the AV indicate the word is not in the Greek at all! The RSV is more literal, simply translating the Greek "speaks in a tongue." Now note the NEB "using the language of *ecstasy.*" (Italics mine.) This is *interpretation,* not *translation.* It goes, as we have previously observed, one step towards a commentary on the Bible.

Consider a third example of literal vs. paraphrase. Hebrews 1:1-2a (AV): "God, who at sundry times and

65

in divers manners spake in time past unto the fathers by the prophets, hath in these last days spoken unto us by *his* Son." The RSV removes the archaisms ("sundry" and "divers") but follows very literally the Greek, "In many and various ways God spoke of old to our fathers by the prophets; but in these last days he has spoken to us by a Son." (Before proceeding, note the facts concerning a charge against the RSV made by some of its critics. The RSV took out "his" Son, emphasized in the Bible (AV), changed it to "a" Son, and so denied the deity of Christ. But look at the facts. "His" in the AV is italicized, meaning not in the Greek at all! The RSV capitalized "Son" in the traditional way of honoring his deity.

J. B. Phillips says, "God, who gave to our forefathers many different glimpses of the truth in the words of the prophets, has now, at the end of the present age, given us the truth in the Son."

Now note the words "glimpses of truth" and "the truth." That is a striking contrast. In my opinion, it properly represents the *meaning* of the author of Hebrews —that God gave the Old Testament worthies "glimpses of truth" but finally and fully gave us "the truth" in His Son! Phillips has again given us, as he so often does, "justifiable paraphrase." His modern speech translation is therefore valuable. But should we treat it in precisely the same way as the more literal RSV?

Consider a fourth example. The AV renders Philippians 3:20, "our conversation is in heaven." Now here the archaism "conversation" is misleading, referring in modern English to "talk" or "dialog between persons." Such talk might be "about" heaven but could it be "in heaven"? The RSV literally renders the Greek, "our commonwealth is in heaven." That is quite a stirring truth. The Christian is a citizen of some country or kingdom on this earth. But our true citizenship (see NEB) is in God's realm. Now observe the "paraphrase" by Dr. Moffatt, "we are a colony of heaven." As a scholar, Dr. Moffatt has noted that Paul was writing to Philippi, a city proud of the fact that it was a "colony" of Rome. (See Acts 16:12, where Luke makes the emphasis that Philippi was a Roman colony.) Now a colony of Rome was supposed to be a "miniature Rome" a "copy of Rome." Roman military garrisons kept order. Roman law was strictly observed. Dr. Moffatt feels Paul was making an analogy for the Philippians, "the church is the colony of heaven on earth." This paraphrase may correctly interpret Paul (see commentaries for different views), but the fact of paraphrase must indeed be noted.

The Combination Version

We should now consider a third category of version, the combination. This is the translation called The Amplified Bible. It differs from the standard versions and the modern speech versions in these two respects:

1. The Amplified Bible is translated by a committee, like the standard. But that committee was not chosen from the same wide distribution of denomination and theological perspective as the committees for the ASV, RSV, and NEB. It was the avowed interest of the publishers to collect the committee to represent "conservative scholarship." This purpose was excellent and the resulting translation has many excellencies. But the reader still ought to have in mind the particular perspective of the committee.

2. The Amplified Bible frequently gives a number of renderings, side by side, and the first one or two of these

come from the already published standard versions, with the "Amplifying committee" adding a few more. The best illustration of this is John 14:16: "And I will ask the Father, and He will give you another Comforter (Counselor, Helper, Intercessor, Advocate, Strengthener and Standby) that He may remain with you forever." "Comforter" comes from the AV, "Counselor" from the RSV, "Advocate" from the NEB, "Standby" is similar to Phillips ("Someone else to stand by you"), "Helper" is from Goodspeed. One unique contribution from the Amplified is the word "Strengthener," which was really, in 1611, the connotation of the AV "Comforter." (It is true the Holy Spirit comforts us in times of sorrow, but the Spirit strengthens the Christian at all times.)

Since the Amplified gives seven renderings for the one Greek word *paracletos* in John 14:16, it can be seen as a valuable version for study in one's private reading. It might, however, be confusing in public reading of Scripture to read such a string of cognate words all in a row. Again, John 5:39 is translated, "You search and investigate and pore over the Scriptures . . ." This is a good translation for private study; it would not be a good sentence in public reading.

Are All These Versions Necessary?

Many sincere laymen in the churches of Christendom seriously doubt whether all these contemporary versions— standard or modern speech—are necessary. Those to whom the "Authorized Version *of* the Bible" is *the* Bible —perfect, complete, and eternal—sometimes look either with fear or disfavor upon the many translations. Sometimes this is simply the antipathy to change that people acquire. Sometimes it is the sort of mental lethargy which keeps people from growing in thought, reading, studying, evaluating.

A Further Look at the Authorized Version

Those who think the King James Version is perfect and the twentieth-century translations are unnecessary (or even harmful) ought, in all good conscience, to take a closer look at both. Some opponents of the new translations have appealed emotionally to the traditions and prejudices of thousands of uninformed laymen, have said things which were not true, drawn inferences which were not logically warranted, and left unsaid (or were ignorant of) some very important facts. Remember that Paul said, "Prove all things; hold fast that which is good." The RSV renders, "Test everything; hold fast what is good."

Let us therefore examine some of the claims for or assumptions concerning the AV, and see what the facts are.

The Claim—"The AV is *the Bible;* all else is translation."

The Fact—The AV is one English version of the Bible, not the Bible. The Scriptures were written in Hebrew and Aramaic (OT) and Greek (NT); all else is translation.

Note the title page of the AV: "The Holy Bible, . . . Translated out of the original tongues."

The Claim—"The AV was based on the autographs, the original manuscripts."

The Fact—There are no autographs (original copies) of the thirty-nine books of the Old Testament or of the twenty-seven books of the New Testament now available. We have copies of copies of copies. The fact is that RSV and NEB (and others) go back to third and fourth century manuscripts of the Greek New Testament, whereas

69

the AV—in much of the New Testament—was translated from manuscripts as late as the thirteenth and fourteenth centuries. The twentieth century versions go back a thousand years closer to the originals! In a sense they are "new" Bibles (new translations), but in a very real sense they represent the "oldest" Bible, both in the Hebrew manuscripts of the Old Testament and the Greek manuscripts of the New Testament. In them we come closer to the very words of Jesus, closer to the very words of his apostles. Such facts must not be ignored by Christian believers.

Return to the title page of the King James Version, and note the words "translated out of the *original tongues.*" (Italics, present writer.) Now from this phrase it has been inferred by many uninformed ministers and laymen that the translators of 1611 were claiming that their version was based on the autographs, "original tongues" being taken to mean "original manuscripts." The fact is that the translators were referring to the original *languages* of Scripture, not to original *manuscripts.*

The Claim—"The AV is called the Authorized Version because it (alone) was authorized by the Holy Spirit."

The Fact—The AV was authorized by King James I (hence the alternate title, King James Version) of England. In the days when England was Roman Catholic, the Pope had to authorize (or refuse authorization) the translation of Scripture. Under Henry VIII, the Church of England became a separate church (the Pope would not let Henry divorce his wife, so the king divorced the Pope!), and the king (or queen) became the head of the church, thus taking over the temporal authority, and much of the spiritual authority, formerly held by the Pope.

Every church library should have at least one good his-

70

tory of the English Bible. Or consult your public library. The American Bible Society has a twenty-five cent pamphlet called "A Ready-Reference History of the English Bible." Every Christian layman and minister should own one.

The Claim—"The AV (alone) was 'appointed to be read in the churches.' " (Inference drawn: our modern churches.)

The Fact—Again a false inference has been drawn from words on some title pages. The facts of English history again give the answer. The "appointment" (like the "authorization") was made by the monarch of England, and the "churches" were the parishes of the Church of England.

The habit of divorcing a statement from its context and historical setting, and then placing a new interpretation on it, is again evidenced. The writer knows of a church which, until a few years ago, spelled out in its bylaws that no minister could read a version other than the King James in the pulpit! And this same church proclaimed it had "no book but the Bible, no creed but Christ"! But it was King James I, not Christ, who "appointed" the translation dedicated to himself to be read in the parishes of the Church of England.

The Claim—"The AV is 'God's Bible.' We do not want the 'Revised Bible,' we want 'God's Bible' "

The Fact—As we have seen earlier, the AV is not, in a technical sense, *"the* Bible" but "an English version *of* the Bible." Now note the prejudice against the word *revised*. Persons with such prejudice wish to settle upon (or have already settled upon!) one version, establishing it as infallible, final, and eternal. No revisions! But this again

71

ignores a plain fact, ensconced on the title page of the AV! For that title carries the sentence, "translated out of the original tongues, with the former translations diligently *compared* and *revised*."

The AV was not the first English version of the Bible (that honor goes to Tyndale, in his first printed English New Testament), nor even the first "authorized" version. The translators of 1604-1611 were greatly indebted to their predecessors. (Some parts of the New Testament in the AV are 80-90 percent Tyndale's translations!) Now note the confession of the translators that they not only "compared" all the previous versions, but "revised" them. *The King James Version was the "Revised Standard Version" of 1611!*

How can anyone read that title page, and then turn around and attack the principle of revision? Language changes, words become obsolete, sometimes reverse their meanings. (A subsequent study will note and discuss some of the "archaisms" in the AV.) As time goes by, scholars learn much more about the Hebrew and Greek languages, about the meanings of words in their original *Sitz im Leben.* (This German phrase may be translated "situation in life." It is used in this nontechnical study because the reader who advances to larger studies will encounter it often.) Revisions become necessary, and the AV of 1611 was such a revision.

Now no scholar will deny that the AV was a magnificent translation in its own day. The translators were the top scholars of the time. The felicity of the translation is felt by all and praised by the experts. It is a "monument of English prose." Once having memorized the Psalms, for instance, in the AV, no other translation seems to come even close in beauty. In the more important spiritual perspective, millions of persons have been won to Christ and nourished in their faith by the AV.

But it is not based on autographs, not based on oldest manuscripts, does have many archaisms, does have some noted mistranslations (some of which have been observed in this study, others to be observed), does have some reading difficulties removed in newer versions.

A Further Look at the Revised Standard Version

When the Revised Standard Version was published (1946, 1952), a barrage, or series of barrages, of vituperative charges were hurled against it. Now, in a way, this was to be expected, for new translations always have called down the storms of attack and require a number of years for balance and good judgment to prevail.

Even the Authorized Version, still so beloved in some circles, was viciously attacked by the Puritans of seventeenth-century England. They accused it of "bad grammar, bad scholarship, bad theology," and besides they did not like it! They adopted the Geneva Version (translated in Geneva, Switzerland) as their "Bible," and it was the Geneva Bible the Pilgrims brought to America in 1621.

The present writer was beginning his teaching ministry in 1946, and he was—and is—appalled at the ferocity of the attacks, the misinformation or lack of information, the hurling of unfounded epithets. Some pamphlets attacking the new version obviously were written by unbalanced people, but even these pamphlets gained wide acceptance in conservative circles. Some critiques were written by supposedly educated men, in a position to find the facts if they had them not, and the innuendoes and distortions were therefore inexcusable.

Since more than twenty years have passed, it may now

be believed by some that the charges and innuendoes have "picked up their tents like Arabs, and silently stolen away." But as the present writer lectures across the country, he discovers many of the old charges are still accepted as "proved" or "true" by many sincere Christians, and this is tragic.

In a class conducted the day before these words were typed, a wonderful and sweet-spirited Christian lady admitted that years ago she had heard a charge against Dr. James Moffatt, and never since would read his version! (The charge was unfounded.) Large numbers of people evidently have never read, or heard, some of the plain facts which dispel the gross charges. This study therefore will deal with some of them, at least in brief.

The Claim—"The translators (RSV) are Communists; the RSV is a Communist Bible."

The Facts—It is easy, so dreadfully easy, to sling the slur of "Communist!" and it takes time and effort to investigate the facts. No member of the translating committee has ever been proved, by reputable authorities in legal session with constitutional safeguards, to be either a member of the Communist Party, or even to espouse any of the major principles of Marxist-Leninist-Stalinist political philosophy! Then how do these charges arise? The following true story may illustrate.

Dr. E. Stanley Jones, noted evangelical preacher whose books and sermons all extol Jesus Christ as Lord, Son of God, Savior (to the personal knowledge of thousands of readers of this story), wrote some years ago a devotional Lenten series for a Detroit newspaper. A reader protested, writing, "Did you not know Dr. E. Stanley Jones was a Communist?" Upon inquiry, it was found her grounds for this charge were: "He wrote a book *on* Communism."

Some time later the present writer visited and reminisced with a high school debating colleague, one known for logic and research. The friend claimed Dr. Jones was a Communist, and when asked for proof, said, "He wrote a book on Communism." The writer asked his friend if he had read the book, had even seen it, had even looked up its title. The friend admitted he had done none of these things. The writer then told him the title, *Christ's Alternative to Communism.* (Note the second word in the title.) So that is the way most of these rumors start concerning noted theologians.

The present writer sat in classes with several of the scholars on the translating team, and has read dozens of books by several of the others, and there is not a Communist in the group! (One brief epilog: the writer bound his copy of the RSV, a presentation copy from a congregation in Scranton, Pennsylvania, in *maroon* imitation leather. Sure enough, a critic pointed to the "red" cover and said the person carrying it had to be Communist!)

The Claim—"The 'revisers' have done away with the deity of Christ."

The Facts—The inferences drawn, without scholarly investigation, from some changes from the AV to the RSV were truly serious, but truly fantastic. Consider one: In Hebrews 1:2 the AV has *"his Son"* ("his" referring to God), the RSV changed to "a Son," so they denied the deity. But the italics in the AV mean, as you have learned, the word was not in the Greek. The Greek is anarthrous (without the article), so the RSV translated "a Son." But notice "Son" in capital letters in the RSV, the customary sign of reverence for the deity of Christ. Early editions of the RSV translated "a son of God" in Mark 15:39 (because the Greek is without the article and because it is not definite, in context, that the centurion became a Christian). However, subsequent editions have, "the Son of God."

We are looking at the charge that the RSV has destroyed, or sought to destroy, the doctrine of the deity of Christ. The reader can check the fallacy of this charge by looking up the phrase "the Son of God" (or "the Son") in a concordance, tracing the phrase through the New Testament in the AV, and then the RSV. Where the Greek has the definite article and calls Jesus "the Son of God" this is preserved intact in the RSV. Where there is no definite article, but where the context clearly indicates Jesus is calling himself (or is being called) "Son" in the unique sense, this is preserved in the RSV. (Just as one test case involving several verses, read John 5:17-47. Again and again, in the RSV, Jesus refers to his unique relationship to the Father.)

There even is one text in the RSV, which its attackers conveniently overlooked, where the Lord is called "God" in the RSV, and not in the AV! Compare Titus 2:13: (AV) "Looking for that blessed hope, and the glorious appearing of the great God and our Savior Jesus Christ"; (RSV) "awaiting our blessed hope, the appearing of the glory of our great *God and Savior* Jesus Christ." (Italics present writer's.) The RSV offers the AV rendering as an alternate translation in the margin, but put in the text a stronger affirmation of Christ as God than there is in the AV.

The Claim—"The RSV has taken away the blood atonement."

The Facts—When the RSV was first attacked in 1946, this claim was frequently made. Most speakers and writers made the charge on the basis of a false inference drawn

76

from the RSV rendering of Colossians 1:14. The AV had translated, "[dear Son] in whom we have redemption through his blood, even the forgiveness of sins." The RSV translated, "in whom we have redemption, the forgiveness of sins." The RSV had clearly omitted, *at this text,* the words "through his blood."

Attackers immediately concluded two things: (1) the omission had been deliberate, and (2) the omission had been complete in the New Testament. One early pamphlet made the blanket statement, "They have taken away the blood atonement." But what are the facts? If the reader of the RSV will continue to Colossians 1:20, he will find the rendering "through him to reconcile to himself all things, whether on earth or in heaven, making peace *by the blood* of his cross" (italics present writer's). If it had been the intention of the revisers to remove references to the blood, they surely did a careless job. No, the critics read one verse, misunderstood the reasoning behind that verse, closed the Bible without reading six verses farther on, and made the charge!

Now turn to Ephesians 1:7 in the RSV and note, "In him we have redemption *through his blood,* the forgiveness of our trespasses." (italics present writer's). If the revisers included the phrase at Ephesians 1:7 (and over thirty other texts), why did they "omit" the phrase at Colossians 1:14? The answer is simple: the *oldest Greek manuscripts* of the Colossian letter do not have the phrase at Colossians 1:14! Later manuscripts added the phrase, probably by memory of some scribe thinking of Ephesians 1:7.

Thirty-four times the Westcott and Hort Greek Testament (based upon earlier rather than later Greek manuscripts) has references to our salvation by the blood of

Jesus, and thirty-four times it is so translated in the RSV. The charge, "they have taken away the blood atonement," was patent nonsense to anyone who would take the trouble to ascertain the facts.

The Claim—"They have taken away the 'divine pronoun' and denied the deity of Christ."

The Facts—The AV translates Matthew 16:16, the words of Peter to Jesus, *"Thou art* the Christ, the Son of the living God" (italics present writer's). The RSV translates the same verse, *"You are* the Christ, the Son of the living God" (italics present writer's). The inference was drawn that *thou* is a divine pronoun used when addressing deity, *you* is a human pronoun used when addressing humanity, therefore the RSV was denying the deity of Christ! As in the case of Colossians 1:14, 20, the answer is only a few verses away, for in the AV of Matthew 16:18 Jesus said to Peter, "Thou art Peter . . ." If *thou* were a sacred pronoun directed to deity, Christ would not so have addressed Peter.

The facts again are simple, and easily ascertained: thee, thou, thine, are not divine pronouns but archaic pronouns, used for you (singular), you (plural), and yours. (Note: many persons, including the present writer, still prefer to use the archaic pronouns in prayer on the premise that God is our Father, but he is still God and ought to be addressed in unique language. But this is personal practice, and has nothing to do with some pronouns being sacred and others not.) The Greek New Testament has no sacred pronoun, *su* is used to address God or man.

It is also to be observed that the RSV, supposedly denying the deity of Christ, has the exact formula "the Son of the living God" which is found in the AV.

78

Attributes of Twentieth-Century Standard Versions

Remember that by standard versions we mean those which are (1) translated by committees of scholars and (2) generally more literal renderings. This category includes the AV (1611), ERV (1881-1885), ASV (1901), RSV (1946-1952), and NEB (1961, 1970).

Previously, we have looked at certain characteristics of the AV and certain characteristics of the RSV. At this point it will be profitable to examine the major differences between all the twentieth-century standard versions, taken as a whole, and the AV of 1611. These differences, in some cases, will be major advantages to the layman as he studies his Bible. Instead of spelling out each time "twentieth-century versions," we shall merely cite RSV-NEB as exemplars of the remainder.

1. *RSV-NEB are based on the oldest extant Greek manuscripts of the New Testament, oldest extant Hebrew manuscripts of the Old Testament.*

This is a far more important fact than the average layman, with no knowledge of Greek or Hebrew, realizes. Since we have no autographs (original writings), it is imperative that we get as close to the originals as possible. No reputable scholar will defend the fourteenth-century manuscripts of the New Testament used by Erasmus in his printed Greek testament, and hence by the translators of 1611, as being as close to the original (either in time or content) as the great codices of the fourth century, the Vaticanus and the Sinaiticus.

As the RSV and NEB are based on much older manuscripts, sometimes there will be "omissions" from the AV and sometimes "differences" from the AV, in text rather than translation. Let us illustrate. In the AV, Mark 16:1-20 is printed as though the entire chapter were equally

79

valid in manuscript evidence. In the RSV and NEB (and many others) Mark 16:9-20 is either put in the margin or by some device indicated as not in the earliest copies of Mark. Most scholars believe the "autograph" of Mark could not have ended at 16:9, "they said nothing to anyone, for they were afraid." There must have been a resurrection ending.

But other copies of Mark, earlier than the fourteenth century manuscripts used by AV, have a shorter ending (see RSV margin). Now here is the point: our English translations should show, at least in major areas, something of the status of the Greek text, and where the earliest manuscripts differ, modern readers have the right to know.

Again, the reader of the RSV and NEB will look in vain for the text printed in the AV as 1 John 5:7, "There are three that bear record in heaven, the Father, the Word, and the Holy Ghost: and these three are one." This text occurs in no ancient Greek manuscript of 1 John. No one therefore has the right to infer that the revisers have "dropped the text" in order to deny the doctrine of the Trinity. (See Matthew 28:19 in both RSV and NEB for the "trinitarian formula" of baptism.)

Because they are based on the oldest extant manuscripts, the RSV and NEB will at points have a major difference (rather than an omission) from the AV. An excellent case in point is Romans 8:28. The AV has, "all things work together for good to them that love God." Note the change in the RSV, "in everything, God works for good with those who love him." The NEB has, "he (the Spirit) cooperates for good with those who love God," and, in the margin, "God himself cooperates for good with those who love God."

In the AV "things" is the subject of the sentence, and

80

we are told "all things work together for good." The earliest manuscripts have "God" (or "the Spirit") as subject, and "in everything God works for good with those who love him." This is not a matter of two different translations of the same Greek manuscript, but a matter of two different manuscripts. The oldest gives a much clearer idea of God's providential workings, even in life's tragedies, which do not—themselves—work for good.

2. *RSV-NEB give at hundreds of points better translations of the original languages.*

Several of these have been noted previously, but there are literally hundreds of places where the new translations are eminently superior. Scholars simply know more about the meanings of Hebrew and Greek words than did the translators of 1611—this is a fact and all the emotional attachments in the world are not going to change it. The new translations take the reader closer, much closer, to the very words of Jesus and of Paul, and much closer to the meanings of those words. Jesus said, "You search the scriptures," not "Search the scriptures" in John 5:39. He said, "Do not be anxious about tomorrow," not "Take therefore no thought for the morrow" in Matthew 6:34. He spoke to the disciples of "my blood of the covenant" (some manuscripts have "new covenant") not "my blood of the new testament" in Mark 14:24.

3. *RSV-NEB remove hundreds of archaisms from the AV.*

An archaism is a word whose meaning is now obsolete, or radically changed. Previously we noted the improved translations in the RSV and NEB. But in the case of the archaisms, the translation was perfectly acceptable in 1611, but is no longer so, because of a word which has radically changed in meaning.

In the AV of Romans 1:13 Paul is made to say, "I purposed to come unto you (but was let hitherto)." Now "let" in modern English is used for *allow* or *permit* and "I purposed to come . . . (but was let)" does not make sense. The RSV "prevented" does make sense. Now take the word *prevent*. It was used in AV of 1 Thessalonians 4:15, "We which are alive and remain [unto the coming of the Lord] shall not prevent them which are asleep" (brackets present writer's). *Prevent* today means *hinder*. How could the Christians awaiting Christ's return hinder those who had died? But in 1611 prevent meant *go before, precede,* and so the RSV correctly translates "precede."

The present writer was puzzled to read as a child that they brought the head of John the Baptist into Herod's palace "in a charger" (Matt. 14:8), for to him "charger" meant war horse. But in 1611 "charger" was good English for "platter" (RSV). The AV rendered 1 Corinthians 15:33, "Evil communications corrupt good manners." Today, "communications" refers to radio and telephone, and "manners" refers to table etiquette. Was that what Paul was talking about? No! He said plainly, "Bad company ruins good morals" (RSV). Our young people need to be told that, plainly and persistently. But will they get that from "evil communications corrupt good manners"?

The AV quotes Paul in 1 Thessalonians 5:14, "Comfort the feebleminded." Now it certainly is important to care for the mentally deficient, the mentally damaged. But that is not what Paul said in Greek. He said, "Encourage the fainthearted" (RSV, NEB).

Paul did not say, "Abstain from all appearance of evil" (1 Thess. 5:22, AV), for that is impossible. He did say, "Abstain from every form of evil" (RSV). (Compare the NEB, "Avoid the bad of whatever kind.")

Paul did not say in Philippians 3:20, "Our conversation is in heaven" (AV). He did say, "Our commonwealth is in heaven" (RSV), or "We . . . are citizens of heaven" (NEB).

Paul was not referring to "conversation" (talk, discourse, dialog) in Philippians 1:27 "Let your conversation be as it becometh the gospel of Christ" (AV). The literal Greek *politeuesthe* means "live as citizens" in the gospel of Christ. The RSV comes close, "Let your manner of life be worthy" and so does the NEB "Let your conduct be worthy. . . ."

Earlier, we noted the removal of the archaisms thee, thou, and thine in the RSV when conversations with the incarnate Christ are reported (see Matthew 16:16, 18 in AV and RSV). These are retained, however, when God is addressed in prayer (see John 17:1ff, RSV) because this is quite customary today in many churches.

4. *RSV-NEB give alternate text possibilities in footnotes.*

This at first may seem a minor point, as many people never pay any attention to footnotes. But the premise of an accurate translation is to give the English reader the equivalent of the Greek (in New Testament), and where two ancient Greek manuscripts differ on which Greek word was employed, it is only honest and accurate to report this in English. Let us illustrate.

Romans 5:1 (AV) reads, "Therefore being justified by faith, we have peace with God." The RSV follows the AV here (the principle of the 1946-1952 translators was to stay as close to the AV as possible, differing only where absolutely necessary) in the text, "we have peace." But there is a marginal reference, "Other ancient authorities read *let us.*"

Now this is not a difference in translation, but in two

Greek texts. One reads *echomen,* "we have peace." But another reads *echōmen,* the subjunctive mode, "let us have peace." The only difference between the two words in Greek is that one has the omicron, short *o* and the other has omega, the long *o*. Now note: no scholar on this earth knows which word Paul dictated to Tertius in the autograph! The claim of verbal inspiration (in the dual sense that God dictated every word and we know which word he dictated!) simply breaks down when the facts are known—and at least some of the facts can be known in the new versions.

Another interesting case where the Greek manuscripts differ by only one letter in a word is 1 Corinthians 13:3. The AV has "though I give my body to be burned." The RSV, true to the principle of following the AV where possible, renders the same "body to be burned." But again in the RSV there is a marginal reference, "Other ancient authorities read *body that I may glory.*" The Greek words differ only in one letter, *kauchesomai* and *kauthesomai.* No scholar knows which Paul wrote (or dictated). Either fits the context.

5. *RSV-NEB give alternate translations in footnotes.*

The RSV uses the phrase "other ancient authorities" to designate other Greek manuscripts, while the NEB uses the phrase, "some witnesses." Keep in mind these are not alternate translations of the same Greek text, as though we had autographs or as though all our copies were identical.

But in the majority of cases the ancient Greek manuscripts do have the same word; but this still does not indicate absolute certainty, because the same Greek word frequently can be translated in two or more ways. Where most of the members of the committee (one of the advantages of the standard versions) agree on a single rendering, it goes into the text (body of translation), but where a majority (or sizable minority) notes that an alternate translation should be offered, this is put in the footnotes.

Paul sometimes called himself, according to the AV, a "servant" of the Lord (as in Titus 1:1). The RSV follows that rendering, but puts "or *slave*" in the margin (footnotes). Now *doulos* in the Greek of Paul's day meant *slave*. The modern connotation of servant misses this meaning, because a servant (employee) is free in the evening, may own his own home, live where he wishes, and so on. A slave in Paul's world had none of these privileges. Paul willingly had become a slave of the Lord, and did not consider himself his own master. The present writer feels *doulos* should be translated *slave* and *servant* (now misleading) dropped entirely. But at least the RSV improves the AV by putting the word in the margin.

A great many leaders missed the marginal rendering, the alternate translation "virgin" at Isaiah 7:14. "Young woman" is put in the text for many lexical, historical, and exegetical reasons we cannot now go into, but critics of the RSV had no right to take to pulpit and printing press to charge, "They have taken 'the virgin birth' out of the Bible." Read Matthew 1:23 in the RSV: "A virgin shall conceive." Read Luke 1:27 in the RSV: "To a virgin . . . and the virgin's name was Mary." Read the RSV alternate rendering at Isaiah 7:14, "or *virgin.*" How tragic that, because of such charges, hundreds of thousands of sincere (but rather gullible) laymen have been kept from the thousands of biblical truths in the new versions!

Note the familiar phrase in the Lord's Prayer (more accurately, the Disciples' Prayer for Jesus gave it to the

85

disciples as a model), "Give us this day our daily bread." Both RSV and NEB have alternate translations in the footnotes, "our bread for the morrow." (Compare Barclay, "bread for the coming day.")

Matthew 6:27 (AV) quotes Jesus as saying, "Which of you by taking thought can add one cubit unto his stature?" The RSV removes the archaism "taking thought" and truly translates the Greek, "by being anxious." It also drops "unto his stature" and substitutes "span of life," because few people (except basketball players) wish to add eighteen inches to their height! But "stature" is indeed a possible rendering of the Greek, so the revisers put it in the margin as an alternate translation.

At the important text in Galatians 2:16, theme and thesis of the letter, the RSV records Paul as saying (essentially with the AV), "A man is not justified by works of the law but through faith in Jesus Christ." There is a marginal reference at "justified," with the alternate translation in the footnotes, "or *reckoned righteous.*" The Greek *dikaioo* is capable of several renderings, and it is important for the English reader to understand that justification by faith basically means we are treated as (reckoned) righteous even though we have not been so. The TEV says we are "put right" with God through our faith in Christ.

6. *RSV-NEB breaks the English text into paragraphs for easier reading and comprehension.*

Most editions of the AV do not paragraph biblical material, and people therefore read contiguous verses as though each was isolated, like separate pearls on a string. This kind of reading would be most intelligible in a collection of proverbs, but even in the Old Testament Book of Proverbs the thought continues through more than one verse and ought to be read in paragraphs (see RSV or NEB).

Older editions of the AV used the printer's sign for a paragraph (¶), but then did not form the paragraph! Most readers either overlooked its presence completely, or did not know what it stood for. And the person who put in the symbols quit in the Book of Acts, and in Paul's letters, where paragraphing is so important, there is no indication whatever. (Those who regularly read the AV should be aware of the English Reference Bible, published by the American Bible Society. It modernizes spelling, consistently spells proper names, indents for poetic portions, sets out sensible paragraphs with section headings, and includes concordance.)

The RSV and NEB provide sensible paragraphing throughout the Bible, in addition to their other contributions.

Review and Conclusions on the Use of the Versions

In closing the chapter on English versions of the Bible, a few suggestions may be in order. These come out of many years of studying, teaching, and preaching from the Hebrew of the Old Testament and the Greek of the New Testament. They have been shared with thousands of people in hundreds of class sessions and Bible conferences, and many ministers and laymen have put them to the test and found them useful in Bible reading and interpretation. I claim no finished finality for them, but believe they will be helpful.

1. Use twentieth-century standard versions of the Bible as your norm.

Either the RSV or NEB will serve this purpose I recommend the RSV in first place and the NEB in second place because the latter more often resorts to paraphrase which interprets the original language rather than merely translating it. There is a fine line of distinction here, but one which should be noted if the reader is unacquainted with the original languages. Consider 1 Corinthians 14:2 as a case in point. The AV has "he that speaketh in an *unknown* tongue." Note the italics. The uninformed person can infer, on the seemingly good ground of modern English usage, that the word *unknown* is italicized because it is to be emphasized. But the opposite is true.

As has been noted earlier, italicized words in the AV are not in the Greek at all! Now the RSV follows the literal Greek, "One who speaks in a tongue." There is no adjective in the Greek, and none is supplied in English. But note the NEB, "When a man is using the language of ecstasy." This is an interpretation, rather than a strict translation, of Paul's words, and thus in my opinion ought to go in a commentary on the text rather than into the text itself. (A subsequent chapter will be devoted to the use of Bible commentaries.)

We noted earlier that the modern speech versions frequently resort to paraphrase rather than literal translation. There is a proper place for this, especially when we remember that each modern speech version represents one scholar's opinion. Many scholars are of the opinion Paul was indeed referring to some esoteric (NEB, ecstatic) language bestowed upon the believer by the Holy Spirit, but this interpretation should go into a commentary rather than into a translation.

The careful reader will observe that many religious publications now quote the Bible very frequently in the RSV, and the RSV is also used for the printed text of Scripture in the church school quarterlies of many denominations, either replacing or appearing side by side with the AV. Even in conservative circles where there was once widespread criticism and condemnation of the RSV, this version is now widely used as a study Bible.

The best study Bible edition of the RSV is the *Oxford Annotated Edition,* and it is recommended to the reader that he purchase the edition which includes the Apocrypha.

2. Use the many excellent modern speech versions to supplement your reading of the standard version(s), thus providing variety of interpretation and freshness of point of view.

One of the benefits here is that when the reader discovers two or more translations of the same Greek word—especially when they are widely divergent—it will pique his curiosity and summon him to further careful Bible study. He will be led to compare still other versions, and see how many scholars agree on a certain translation. He will be led to the commentary in an effort to find out why the translators disagree. He will develop the habit of reading the context to see what light it throws on the verse in question. (Review, for instance, John 5:38 and note the light it throws on the translations of AV and RSV at John 5:39.) He will look up other passages with the same word to see what other New Testament passages have to say. The supplementary use of modern speech versions can be an excellent stimulus to careful Bible study, to exegesis rather than eisegesis.

3. Use the AV for some of its time-honored expressions and acknowledged beauty of language.

Educated people will pay tribute to the AV as a monument of English prose as long as the English language endures upon the earth. As the lover of literature reads

Blake, Whittier, Emerson, Thoreau, Lincoln, Churchill, he hears the echoes of the King James Version of the Bible. Some people always will prefer the sonorous phrases of the AV in the hour of liturgy, whatever they prefer in the private study.

4. Remember that we are redeemed by our Lord Jesus Christ, regardless of the versions which leads us to him.

This point cannot be overstressed. The Bible has been translated into almost all of the languages spoken by man on this earth, and the same gracious promise of eternal life is extended to all. Man may read John 3:16 in Urdu, in Hindi, in Spanish, in Swahili, in German, in English— it does not matter. The promise of God's good grace will reach him, and if he responds to God he will be saved.

So often in Christian history we have emphasized the minutiae which divide us rather than the message which unites us. We have crystallized a translation or a tradition, we have canonized and creedalized and bent into endless conformities. But there is "One God and Father of us all, who is above all and through all and in all" (Eph. 4:6). Scholars will differ whether Paul wrote these words or a disciple wrote in his name, they will differ in the way they translate the Greek of the Ephesian letter, and they will argue minute interpretations of this or that verse. But the words of Scripture, whatever the translation, do indeed bring us to the grace of God in Christ.

4

The Use of Concordance and Commentary

The Use of the Concordance

1. *Definition* The concordance gives an alphabetical listing of the principal words in a book, here, the Bible, with immediate context (limited) of each.

2. *Some Important English Concordances*

a) Large, complete. The two best concordances for the AV are (1) Young, *Analytical Concordance* and (2) Strong, *Exhaustive Concordance*. For reasons given below, Young is recommended, but both have ample indexes of biblical words.

There is a complete concordance available for the RSV. It is published by Nelson. It does not give the transliterations for Greek and Hebrew words in the manner of Young and Strong. For the minister, church school teacher, or layman who can afford only one large concordance, Young is recommended. When the text is looked up in Young, the RSV then can be compared.

It may be of interest to learn that Young and Strong required an entire generation of their lives to look up and index all the occurrences of the words of the Bible. In the case of the RSV concordance, the words were fed into a computer, and the listings were completed in hours!

At the present writing there is no complete concordance for the entire Bible in the NEB, as the Old Testament portion was only recently published. Such a concordance undoubtedly will be on the market soon.

91

b) Small, desk size. Here the most popular concordance is Cruden. Being smaller, it does not give nearly as many occurrences of each word listed. Comparison should be made between Cruden and the two large concordances, Young and Strong, to ascertain the degree of helpfulness rendered. It is recommended that every church library own the Young's Analytical.

For the pastor or layman who wishes a complete library, there are concordances available on some of the modern speech translations, such as Moffatt. Check with your bookstore or publisher.

3. *The Two Main Uses of the Concordance*

The first is by far the most common: to look up a passage of Scripture whose location you have forgotten. Suppose the minister preached last Sunday from the text, "They that wait upon the Lord shall renew their strength; they shall mount up with wings as eagles; they shall run, and not be weary; and they shall walk, and not faint." You wish to turn to your Bible during the week and reread that magnificent promise, but you have forgotten where it is found! You can look in the concordance under "wait" or "Lord" or "renew" or "strength"—any important word—and discover that the text occurs at Isaiah 40:31. This type of follow-up on the scriptural passages heard in church is recommended to laymen. Your knowledge of the Bible will be much more systematic and much more complete if you make a regular practice reading the biblical passage which was preached upon the Sunday before.

The second use of the concordance is much less frequently employed, and there are some recommendations which should be made at this point. That is to *trace an important theological term, as "save," "sanctify," "justify," through a book, or several books, of the Bible*. This requires some time and some work, and many therefore will ignore it! But those who follow the suggestion will discover new vistas of truth opening before their eyes, and place biblical doctrines in profound perspectives the person never knew existed. It gives broader views of Christian doctrine, saves us from half-truths and from selecting part of the evidence (that which seems to accord with what we already think!), and reveals some of the profound paradoxes of the Bible.

Let us illustrate. Salvation is a most important biblical theme. But is *salvation* (1) a past actualization, something which happened back there when we met the Lord, so that we can say, "I *have been* saved"? Or (2) is it a future consummation, to happen in heaven, "we *shall be* saved"? Or (3) is it a present realization, a process instead of an act, so that one says, "I *am being* saved"?

Some Christians would select the first, some the second, some the third. And like the "blind men of Indostan" in the famous poem, each of whom felt part of the elephant and came away to report what he thought to be the "whole truth," each group would be partially right and partially wrong. Now trace the verb *save* in the concordance. You find: (1) a past actualization, Ephesians 2:8, "by grace you *have been saved.*" (RSV). But also (2) a future consummation, Matthew 10:22, "he who endures to the end *shall be saved.*" But also (3) present realization, 1 Corinthians 1:18 (RSV), "The word of the cross is folly to those who are perishing, but to us who *are being saved* it is the power of God."

The Bible Commentary

In a good twentieth-century version of the Bible, you have a fairly accurate idea of what Jesus (or Paul, or

James) *said,* but this needs to be supplemented by a tool which will give further knowledge of what they *meant.* People frequently ask, "Does the Greek throw any light on such texts as 'if your right hand causes you to sin, cut it off and throw it away'?" The answer has to be no for our English versions all faithfully render the Greek at this point, and that is definitely what Jesus said. But no mentally balanced person will think this is literally what Jesus meant. But some will reply, "Granted, we know what Jesus did not mean. But what did he mean?"

This question clearly shows the need of the third tool of exegesis (after the version and the concordance), the commentary. In an earlier part of the present study, we encouraged the student of Scripture to ask the questions: Who said this? Who wrote the book in which it was said? What did he say? What did he mean? When and where did he say it? Why? To whom? The answers to some of the questions can be supplied in part by a good version and by logical, deductive reasoning. But many answers come only from the commentary.

But what commentary (ies)? Aye, there's the rub! Some scholars are hesitant to recommend any commentary to laymen, because laymen so often infer that the scholar therefore agrees with *all the ideas* in the commentary, and this means trouble! Perhaps the present writer is a "fool who rushes in where angels fear to tread." But, with great respect for all who differ, he feels certain recommendations, with stated limitations, can and should be made, and that laymen will benefit from intelligent use of certain commentaries now available. Readers please note: *the recommendation of the following commentaries does not indicate this writer agrees with all the statements in any one of them.* With this caveat, let us proceed.

94

1. *A Brief List of One-Volume Commentaries*

The following one-volume commentaries (on the Bible, or on Old or New Testament) will be found helpful: Jamieson-Fausset-Brown (abridgement of larger, multi-volume work), Abingdon, Dummelow, Peake (new edition, edited by Rowley and Black), Wycliffe, *Twentieth-Century Commentary, Old Testament Commentary* (ed. Alleman and Flack). Two things, in general, ought to be noted:

a) Since one volume covers the entire Bible, or one of the Testaments, the treatment necessarily is brief. Comments sometimes will be general comments on entire paragraphs, and the particular verse you are interested in may not be treated at all. Before purchasing one of these, it is a good idea to note some test passages in a library copy. (Even small towns now are beginning to develop good libraries, and Bible students should take advantage of the increasingly good religious books sections.) Put two or three commentaries on the table before you, then consult each and note the relative value for yourself.

b) Another general comment: the student should balance his reading between more *conservative* and more *liberal* commentaries. Now these appelations are not precise (hence the italics), but, generally, the *conservative* interpreter will follow Christian tradition more closely, where the *liberal* will feel free to depart from tradition at a number of points.

As with *conservatism* and *liberalism* in politics, there are many hues in the theological spectrum, and no definitive comment can be made. But the reader ought to learn something of the theological background of each commentary, and balance his reading accordingly. *The Abingdon Bible Commentary* would, at points, represent various

95

degrees of liberal scholarship; the *Wycliffe Bible Commentary* would represent the more conservative approach.

2. *A Brief List of Multi-Volume Commentaries*

Beacon Commentaries, Cambridge Commentary (on *The New English Bible.* Do not confuse with the older *Cambridge Bible for Schools and Colleges,* which is older, but still good.), *Daily Study Bible* (William Barclay, the New Testament only), *The Interpreter's Bible* (massive twelve volume set), *The Layman's Bible Commentary,* the *New International Commentary* (OT and NT), *The Tyndale Commentaries,* the *Wesleyan Bible Commentary,* and A. T. Robertson's *Word Pictures in the New Testament.*

Again we urge that volumes be consulted in a library or bookstore before purchase is made, and also urge the balance between liberal and conservative scholarship.

The Interpreter's Bible has many liberal commentators in the set, but an enormous amount of valuable historical, archeological, and exegetical information makes it valuable, and the settled Christian can recognize the extremes of liberalism when he meets them. The IB ought to be balanced by the NICOT (*New International Commentary, OT*) and the NICNT (*New International Commentary, NT*). The scholarship is superb, and the viewpoint basically conservative.

The following general observations may be made on the use of commentaries.

1. Ascertain the dates of publication, and use newer as well as older commentaries.

In teaching Bible conferences, the writer is amazed to learn how many people use commentaries as indiscriminately as they use versions, asking no questions about origin or significance. We have noted earlier that the seventeenth-century translators of the AV were fine scholars, and performed a magnificent work. Yet their work was far from perfect, and it is a fact that scholars now have knowledge of the Greek New Testament which the learned gentlemen of King James's day could not have had. The same general rule applies to commentaries. Adam Clarke and Matthew Henry were fine students of the Bible, and their homilies contain spiritual benefit for modern-day students of the Bible. But much knowledge has come to us since the days of Clarke and Henry, and no Christian inquirer should think of contenting himself with these classic commentaries alone.

Note one case in point. When the present writer pursued his undergraduate studies in religion, he was informed in class lectures and in textbooks that the oldest extant (now available to scholars) manuscript of the Book of Isaiah in Hebrew dated back to the tenth century of the Christian era. But the discovery of the Dead Sea Scrolls in recent years has given us two manuscripts of the Book of Isaiah which are dated by many scholars as early as 200 B.C.! In one archeological discovery, we traveled over a thousand years closer to the "autograph" (original) of the Book of Isaiah.

One thing learned from the comparison of these manuscripts (tenth century A.D. and second century B.C.) is that we have in our Masoretic Text of the Old Testament a substantially accurate record of the ancient originals, even though we do not have a word-for-word corroboration. As it is true that two English versions translated from the same manuscript will differ in some detail, it is also true that the manuscripts themselves differ in some detail. But we do have substantially corroborated records of the ancient Scriptures, and this degree of accuracy is

97

all we need to bring us to the knowledge of God in the Judaeo-Christian Scriptures.

2. Balance your commentary study between conservative and liberal points of view.

Some students of the Bible assume we have, or at least yearn for, one perfect translation which will give us absolute exactitude, and dismiss the need for any other. This is to commit the error of simplicism, wishing that all the problems of the world were reduced to childish dimensions. The mature Christian wants an education in the Bible, not a brainwashing. He therefore must read wisely. He should compare points of view, weigh evidence, evaluate. Only when he compares two extremes can he find his way to a more moderate and sensible point of view. This is true in weighing political and economic theories, and it applies to the investigation of religious ideas.

Consider a case in point. Scholars who teach the New Testament and laymen who study it will agree that The Letter of Paul to the Ephesians is one of the high-water marks of the New Testament. It has within it an ecstasy of the Christian experience and an exaltation of the majesty of Christ which has few peers or parallels. Its doctrine of the church as the bride of Christ (chap. 5) and of the individual Christian as being "filled with all the fulness of God" (Eph. 3:19) is magnificent Christian theology.

But is this letter an authentic production from the hand of Paul, as it claims in text, in title, and in ancient Christian tradition, or was it written by a disciple of Paul? The case for the position that Paul did not write the letter, is argued by Dr. Francis Beare in *The Interpreter's Bible* (Vol. 10, p. 597ff.). The case for the more conservative position is argued by Dr. E. K. Simpson in his commentary in the series *The New International Commentary on the New Testament* (p. 17ff.). The point here is that the mature Christian ought to inform himself on both sides of the question, not one side only.

But when the person without theological training reads two points of view in opposing commentaries, how does he judge between them? In the present writer's opinion, the answer goes back to an important point made earlier in connection with the use of the concordance: trace the important doctrines all the way through the New Testament, and see the united testimony of the evangelists (authors of the four Gospels), of Paul in his letters, of the author of Hebrews, and so on.

3. Use one or more New Testament commentaries which give the transliterated Greek word, as well as its translation. There are many excellent sets which do this, but we call particular attention to three. The first, and latest of the three, is William Barclay, *The Daily Study Bible*. The title sounds like a translation, but it is a set of pocket-sized commentaries on the New Testament books. The second, older but very good, is A. T. Robertson, *Word Pictures in the New Testament* (6 volumes). The third is a series of Bible studies by Kenneth Wuest, such as *Hebrews in the Greek New Testament, Galatians in the Greek New Testament,* and so on.

Let us illustrate the use of these sets. The Apostle Paul used the Greek word *hagiazo* in more than one sense. He called the Corinthians "sanctified" (1 Cor. 1:2) and "saints" (same verse) but elsewhere (as in 1 Thess. 5:23) voiced the prayer that they become sanctified! This might appear to be contradictory.

But if you go to Robertson or Barclay you will be given

the Greek word *hagiazo,* and then be told that it meant first of all to "set a place apart for God" and secondly to "make holy or saintly" that which had been set apart. The Corinthians had indeed been set apart to God in Christ, but they had not yet taken on themselves the moral coloration which that setting apart demanded. Barclay goes on to show (p. 11 in his commentary on Corinthians) how the word *saint* acquired misleading connotations in later days, but in the New Testament was from the same root (*hagios*) as *hagiazo.*

A second illustration of the value of such sets as Barclay and Robertson is seen in Philippians 3:12, 15. In verse 12 Paul disclaims perfection: "Not that I . . . am already perfect" (RSV). The AV also has "perfect" here, and then goes on to translate 3:15 "Let us therefore, as many as be perfect, be thus minded." Now why would Paul say in one verse he was not perfect, and then include himself with those who were perfect?

The untrained reader might think this a contradiction, but actually it is a paradox. In one sense Paul is perfect; in another he is not. (As in one sense we are saved; in another sense we are not—review Eph. 2:8 and Matt. 10:22.) The RSV softens (or removes) the paradox here by translating Philippians 3:12 "Not that I . . . am already perfect." and 3:15, "Let those of us who are *mature* be thus minded." (Several other modern versions use this same translation.)

Now go to the commentary where the Greek is transliterated and explained. Paul's word is *teleios,* and this from *telos,* literally meaning "end." Now this is the clue we need. From the literal meaning "end" the word acquired the derived meaning "goal." (Visualize the "end" of a fencerow; two boys might race for the "end" in which

100

case it becomes their "goal.") This fact gives another clue: there are immediate goals and ultimate goals.

So Paul was saying, in words clear to his Greek speaking audience and clear to us when we understand them, "I am not perfect—I have not arrived at the final goal of my life." But he would also have to say, "We Christians are not mature, we have arrived at some intermediate goals. Such mature Christians wish to press on to the final goal." A. T. Robertson concludes, "Paul has made great progress in Christlikeness, but the goal is still before him."

5

Bible Dictionary and Harmony

The Bible Dictionary-Encyclopedia

Many readers of the Bible ignore for exegesis a tool which is extremely important and quite accessible to them. This is the Bible dictionary-encyclopedia.

Observe in the first place the two differences between the Bible dictionary and the dictionary regularly consulted for definitions of English words (Webster, Funk & Wagnalls, and others). The first important difference is that the latter dictionaries give definitions of words *as they are now used,* rather than definitions and descriptions of Bible words as they were *used in the original contexts.* Consider two brief illustrations.

When you consult the word *church* in the *Webster's Seventh New Collegiate Dictionary,* the first definition you encounter is: "a building for public especially Christian worship." Of course the word *church* has this (among other) connotation today. As these words are written the writer is looking from his office window at the spire of a beautiful church. But in all its occurrences in the New Testament, this word never once refers to a building (except in metaphor)!

Use of a Bible dictionary will quickly reveal to the reader that in the New Testament the word *church* (from the Greek *ecclesia,* "the called out") meant: the body of Christian believers in a local congregation or assembly (see 1 Cor. 1:2), or the total body of believers across the world (see Eph. 5:25).

Or consider the important word *saint,* as in 1 Corinthians 1:2: "To the church of God which is at Corinth, to those sanctified in Christ Jesus, called to be saints." Or Philippians 1:1b: "To all the saints in Christ Jesus who are at Philippi." If the Bible reader turns to Webster (again Seventh Collegiate) for a definition of *saint,* the first definitions he encounters are: "1. one officially recognized as preeminent for holiness especially through canonization, 2a. one of the spirits of the departed in heaven, b. angel. 3a. one of God's chosen people, b. one belonging to the entire company of baptized Christians." Now the first two of these definitions reflect modern usage, and in the first case usage in Roman Catholic, and not in Protestant, circles.

Theologians have the privilege of defining words as they wish, but the Bible reader wants to know, "what did the word *saint* mean to Paul and his readers?" He will find the answer quickly in the Bible dictionary: Saint (Greek *hagios,* "set apart") in the New Testament connotes a person set apart to God in Christ, i.e. a Christian believer. (This is indicated in Webster's third definition.) The careful student of the Bible should observe this principle: consult general dictionaries for current connotations, but study the Bible dictionary-encyclopedia for the original biblical connotations of important theological terms.

The second difference is indicated by the title "Bible dictionary-encyclopedia." The general dictionary gives only one or more brief definitions, while the Bible dictionary-encyclopedia supplies an important article on the subject. Let us illustrate. Read Matthew 16:6, where Jesus said to his disciples, "Beware of the leaven of the Pharisees." Suppose the modern reader of Matthew does not understand this allusion because he knows nothing about

103

the Pharisees. Webster's Seventh identifies: "A member of a Jewish sect of the intertestamental period noted for strict observance of rites and ceremonies of the written law and for insistence on the validity of the oral law." This is a good brief definition, and gives a clue as to the interpretation of Matthew 16:6. But the careful reader of the Bible should consult at least a brief article (as the two-column article in *The New Westminster Dictionary of the Bible*), and for more information a longer article (as the thirteen-column article in *The Interpreter's Dictionary of the Bible,* Vol. 3). Such articles give more historical background, and cite other New Testament texts which throw light on the text being studied.

Three general principles should be observed before the reader uses (and especially before he purchases) a Bible dictionary. The first is to select an up-to-date dictionary, especially for historical subjects. A theological article (one on faith or salvation for example) may have great merit today even though it was written thirty years ago. But a Bible dictionary issued thirty years ago is badly out of date at many points. It would have no article, for instance, on The Dead Sea Scrolls (discovered in 1947).

The second principle is to balance study or consultation of Bible dictionaries, as with Bible commentaries, between the liberal and conservative poles. The educated reader wishes to consider more than one perspective or point of view, especially in theological as opposed to historical articles. One may cite *The Zondervan Pictorial Dictionary of the Bible,* and Unger's *Bible Dictionary,* as excellent exemplars of the more conservative point of view, while *The Interpreter's Dictionary of the Bible,* in at least a few of its theological articles, would represent the more liberal point of view.

The third principle is to note the relative uses and values of the one-volume as opposed to the multi-volume Bible Dictionary. Every serious Bible student should own at least one small Bible dictionary, to be kept at his desk or on his table alongside his Bible version, concordance, and commentary.

Of all the excellent one-volume dictionaries now available, the present writer would suggest *The New Westminster Dictionary of the Bible,* edited by Dr. Henry Snyder Gehman (1970). Dr. Gehman is a great scholar, and his work is balanced in historical and theological perspectives. The best multi-volume dictionary-encyclopedia is the previously cited *Interpreter's Dictionary of the Bible* (4 volumes, 1962).

Harmony of the Gospels

A most important tool for the study of a major segment of the New Testament is the harmony of the (synoptic) Gospels. In conducting Bible conferences and seminars across the country, the writer finds far too few people taking advantage of this splendid source of insight into the words and works of our Lord.

First, two definitions. A harmony of the gospels is a book which prints the text (body) of Matthew, Mark, and Luke in parallel columns. (Do not confuse this with the *chart* commonly called "harmony of the Gospels" which appears in the back of some study Bibles. The chart only cites the references, the harmony actually prints out the passages.)

Again, note the word *synoptic* above. It comes from the Greek for "seeing together," and it is applied in biblical scholarship to Matthew, Mark, and Luke because they seem to "see together" the life of Christ, with John taking a different perspective. (The student should read a chapter on the Synoptic Gospels from a good New Testament introduction, or the article from a good Bible dictionary.) Most modern harmonies therefore print the text of Matthew, Mark, and Luke in parallel columns, hence a "snyoptic harmony."

The writer recommends to Bible students that they purchase the harmony *Gospel Parallels* (Thomas Nelson, second edition, revised, 1957), and that they increase the value of their harmonic studies by underlining the parallel passages with colored pencils as follows:

Identical words in Matthew, Mark, Luke underline in red.

Identical words in Matthew, Mark, _____ underline in blue.

Identical words in Matthew, _____, Luke underline in green

Identical words in _____, Mark, Luke underline in brown

Synonymous words in any of the three, underline in orange

Differing or discrepant words, underline in yellow

Unique words in any of the three, underline in lavender

(Note: the _____ indicates that the gospel does not have that particular word, or has a different word.)

Before you buy a harmony, try out this procedure by typing the text of Matthew 3:7-10 in the left-hand column of a sheet of paper, and the text of Luke 3:7-9 in the right-hand column, balancing the words and sentences opposite each other. Note that the denunciation of John the Baptist (in the RSV), beginning with the words "You brood of vipers" is identical in the Matthean and Lukan records, except for the synonymous words "presume" (Matthew) and "begin" (Luke). Now consult these two passages in a harmony (p. 9 if you are using *Gospel Parallels),* and note that Mark does not have the paragraph at all.

Next, type out the texts (or consult the texts in a harmony) of Matthew 3:13-17 in the left column, Mark 1:9-11 in the center column, and Luke 3:21-22 in the right column. Arrange the words so that the same or similar words are opposite each other. If you are underlining, underline the words *voice, from heaven* in red; they are identical in the three gospels.

But also note the differences. Mark and Luke agree that the voice of God said *to Jesus, "Thou art* my beloved Son; *with thee* I am well pleased" (italics mine), but Matthew reports the voice of God came *to the crowd* and said, *"This is* my beloved Son, with *whom* I am well pleased." The three records are the same in essence, but they do differ in detail. By careful observation—enhanced by the color underlinings suggested—of the many similarities and dissimilarities in the synoptics, the student of the life of Christ can truly understand the gospel records.

There are many advantages in using the harmony, but consider especially the following:

1. It gives a fuller and more detailed picture of any particular incident in the life of Jesus. If we had Mark's record (of the baptism of Jesus) alone, we would miss the fact (reported by Matthew) that John the Baptist demurred, and said, "I need to be baptized by you." Both Matthew and Mark report that the Spirit "descended like a dove" but only Luke has the words *"in bodily form* as a dove" (italics mine).

Or recall the story of the "rich young ruler" (Matt.

107

19:16-30, Mark 10:17-31, Luke 18:18-30). All three report his wealth, but we learn only from Matthew that he was "young" (verse 20), and only from Luke that he was a "ruler" (verse 18). We need the three records, and we need them in parallel columns, and we need to underline in order to discover what the three have in common, and what each contributes uniquely.

2. Such study shows that even where small details differ in the three records, there is independent corroboration of the essentials of the life of Jesus. One extreme interpretation would deny that there are any differences in the record. Another extreme would make too much of minor differences and ignore major agreements. Careful study of the synoptic harmony will help avoid these extremes.

3. The study will show the particular purpose of each Gospel, and the one fundamental purpose of all the gospels. We soon can learn from studying the Gospels in parallel that Matthew emphasizes Jesus' fulfillment of Old Testament prophecies, Mark writes for Gentiles and has to explain Jewish customs (see Mark 7:3), Luke was an educated Gentile and emphasized the universal mission of Jesus (see Luke 3:6, where Luke alone finishes the Old Testament quotation, ". . . and all flesh shall see the salvation of God").

But all three evangelists obviously had the same fundamental purpose: to convince all who read that Jesus is the Christ, the Son of God.

God Speaks Through His Word

In this book we have discussed some of the tools and techniques which will aid the earnest inquirer in his study of the Bible. We have perforce dealt with facts; historical, literary, linguistic. We have discussed many versions of the Bible and weighed their relative advantages. We have looked at the use of the concordance, the commentary, the dictionary-encyclopedia, the harmony of the Gospels. All these tools and techniques have been dedicated to exegesis, the "leading out" of the ideas in the original, rather than eisegesis, the "leading in" of our own ideas.

But such discussions can appear to be cold, or remote from the deep realities of human experience, especially as they appear on the printed page. The writer wishes to close with a testimony of Christian experience, and an exhortation to all other discoverers of Christ the Truth, who apprehends us, and seekers after the truths we may in our humanity apprehend.

I believe the Bible is the inspired word of God. Paul wrote to Timothy that from childhood he (Timothy) had been "acquainted with the sacred writings which are able to instruct . . . for salvation through faith in Christ Jesus. All scripture is inspired by God and profitable for teaching, for reproof, for correction, and for training in righteousness" (2 Tim. 3:15-16). When we study the historical situation and literary context we learn that some of our traditions about this text represent eisegesis rather than exegesis.

109

But the fundamental fact was true for Paul and Timothy, is true for me, and will be found true for every person who believes and follows: the Scripture leads us to the Savior, and the Savior leads us to God. Jesus himself made this claim in John 5:39 and context: men would have to realize that salvation (eternal life) was not to be found in the legalistic practice of old covenant codes, but was to be found in himself! "It is they (the Old Testament books) that bear witness to me," our Lord said, "yet you refuse to come to me that you may have life."

Thousands of truths in the Old Testament are inspiring and edifying and helpful. But I have found life abundant and life eternal in the Christ to whom those passages point. I believe God inspired a man named Moses, and, through Moses, brought into the world the most wonderful knowledge of the one true God that the ancient world possessed. And much of that knowledge is as valid today as it was in the centuries now silent and gone.

But Moses himself predicted that God would "raise up . . . a prophet" whom the people would heed (Deut. 18:15). Moses never said, "All things have been delivered to me by my Father; and no one knows the Son except the Father, and no one knows the Father except the Son and any one to whom the Son chooses to reveal him. Come to me . . . and I will give you rest." But Jesus said these words (Matt. 11:27-28a), and I believe them and have acted on them and have proved them true.

This does not deny Moses' inspiration or depreciate the way he was used of God; it recognizes the truth of John 1:17, "For the law was given through Moses, grace and truth came through Jesus Christ." "Grace" (Greek *charis*, "unmerited favor") has come to me from God through Christ, but Moses helps lead me to Christ. John further says, "No one has ever seen God; the only Son, who is in the bosom of the Father, he has made him known" (John 1:18). The fourth evangelist did not deny the inspiration and value of the testimonies of Old Testament worthies that they had "seen" the one true God, but he did testify that no "seeing" of God by men of old could compare with our "seeing" of God in Christ—and I believe his testimony.

I know from the Greek of Galatians 3:24 (and readers of the English may discover in modern versions) that Paul, a former Pharisee and devotee of the Torah (Law of Moses) did not call that Torah a "schoolmaster" to lead to Christ, leaving silent the role of Jesus, but called it a "custodian" (tutor, slave, attendant) whose role was not to be the final arbiter in religion, not the full and final voice of God to the world, but the tutor who would prepare us for our one great Teacher—Jesus Christ the Son of God.

I was not, like Paul, reared from infancy to keep Sabbath (Saturday) in legalistic strictness, abstain from pork, withhold social concourse from Gentiles, and so on. But I can understand the role of those premises and prohibitions of the old covenant, and I can agree that "A man is not justified by works of the law, but through faith in Jesus Christ . . ." (Gal. 2:16).

Nowhere did Paul deny to the Galatians the inspiration of the Old Testament, but neither did he call it the absolutely perfect and absolutely permanent method by which God would save men. Rather, it would be the attendant who would take us by the hand and lead us to Christ, our Teacher.

Jesus came to "fulfill" Torah, not destroy it (Matthew 5:17). But he fulfilled it not in following its legalistic

111

minutiae, but in giving a higher law, the final will of God for human conduct, "Love your enemies and pray for those who persecute you" (Matt. 5:44).

No Old Testament prophet ever said, "I am the way, and the truth, and the life; no one comes to the Father but by me," but Jesus said it (John 14:6), and I believe it! No one else said, "He who has seen me has seen the Father," but Jesus said it (John 14:9), and I believe it. The evangelist John believed in the inspiration ("God-breathing," "God-influencing") of the Old Testament prophets, but it was of Jesus that he said, "These [signs] are written that you may believe that Jesus is the Christ, the Son of God, and that believing you may have life in his name" (John 20:31). I did—and do—believe, and I did—and do—have life in his name!

I testify that Jesus Christ is the Son of God, the Revelation of the Father. I testify that the Bible, whatever its version, is a reliable record of that revelation, and will lead us to Christ. I exhort all who read these words to follow those Scriptures to find that Christ, praying for the aid of the Paraclete who will, as Jesus promised, "Teach [us] all things."